Because there were fewer aircraft than there were pilots to fly them, no one pilot was assigned exclusive use of a single Spitfire during Beurling's Malta days. The squadron log of 249 shows the Canadian ace flew the Mark Vc designated TZ BR 135 in more combat patrols than any other Spitfire in the squadron. Unofficially, TZ could be called Beurling's airplane at Takali.

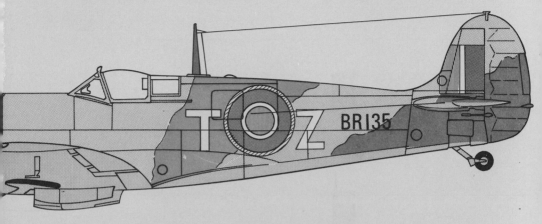

Records show that this is the aircraft, a Vickers-Supermarine Spitfire Mark Vc, which Beurling flew off the aircraft-carrier H.M.S. *Eagle* in Operation "Salient", June 9, 1942, bound for Takali airfield in Malta. Note the extra ninety-gallon long-range fuel tank rigged beneath the aircraft.

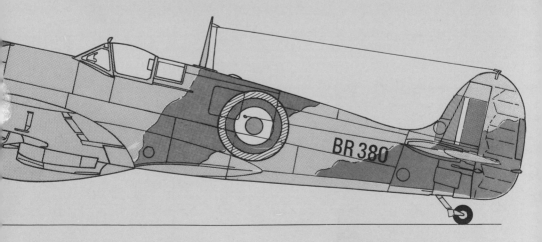

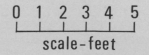

0 1 2 3 4 5
scale–feet

HERO

HERO

The Buzz Beurling Story

BRIAN NOLAN

LESTER
&ORPEN
DENNYS
PUBLISHERS

Canadian Cataloguing in Publication Data

Nolan, Brian.
Hero

Bibliography: p.
Includes index.
ISBN 0-919630-40-5

1. Beurling, Buzz, 1921-1948. 2. Fighter pilots —
Canada — Biography. 3. World War, 1939-1945 —
Aerial operations, Canadian. I. Title.

D792.C2B48   940.54'4971   C81-094432-4

A PEPPERMINT DESIGN / RICHARD MILLER
PRODUCTION / PAULA CHABANAIS

Printed and bound in Canada for
Lester & Orpen Dennys Ltd.
78 Sullivan Street
Toronto, Ontario
MT5 1C1

Contents

Foreword   **xi**

Prologue   **1**

1. The Word of God   **7**

2. Growing Up   **13**

3. Aircraftman No. 1267053, RAFVR   **21**

4. An Island Besieged   **35**

5. Dangerous Flight   **41**

6. Summer at Takali   **51**

7. Coming Home   **77**

8. The Living Legend   **91**

9. Lonely Farewell   **111**

10. The Honeymoon   **115**

11. Dark Peace   **129**

12. The Machal   **137**

13. Death on the Tiber   **149**

14. The Riddle in Rome   **161**

15. A Short, Troubled Life   **171**

Epilogue   **179**

Appendix   **183**

Acknowledgments   **187**

Selected Bibliography   **191**

Index   **195**

The Truth about a man is
first of all what he hides.

André Malraux

For V.M.A.

Foreword

A REPORTER'S CURIOSITY kindled my interest in George Beurling. In 1975, when I was writing and directing a television series for the Canadian Broadcasting Corporation on the history of flight in Canada, Beurling's name (which incidentally is pronounced "*Bur*ling" by the family) and his remarkable feats naturally enough surfaced as the research material piled up.

Beurling had been Canada's greatest hero of the Second World War. He was called the "Falcon of Malta", the "Knight of Malta", a rangy youth who won the Distinguished Service Order, the Distinguished Flying Cross, the Distinguished Flying Medal and Bar—all by the time he was twenty-one years old.

In combat in Malta alone (at the time he was serving in the RAF) he shot down twenty-seven airplanes in a period of just fourteen days. Before the war ended his total had climbed to thirty-one and a third, making him one of the ten best Allied fighter pilots of the Second World War.

Yet, within a generation, his deeds had been forgotten and his name had vanished from the nation's memory. The youngster from Verdun, Quebec, made his last headlines in 1948; he was killed in a plane crash on his way to fight and fly for the new state of Israel. His death was as strange as his life, one shrouded in mystery.

In 1978 I set out on the trail of the Falcon. The search

would take me from the Laurentian Mountains of Quebec to the hills of the Côte d'Azur, from an abandoned airfield in Malta to an airstrip on the banks of the Tiber River. Along the way I talked to hundreds of people in an effort to document the life of this extraordinary pilot, an almost mythical figure largely ignored in Canadian history.

I am grateful to those many people who have contributed to this examination, but I must accept final responsibility for the portrait of Beurling as it emerges in this book.

THE HOMESTEAD
North Onslow, Quebec
February, 1981

HERO

Prologue

TAKALI AIRFIELD, Malta. The summer of 1942.

The atmosphere of the island is surreal: a lime green sky at dawn and pastel butterflies flitting about between the falling bombs.

Of course it is utter madness.

In a hut beside the runway someone is playing an Al Bowlly phonograph record, a ballad promising moonlight and love.

Then there are the lizards. They burrow crazy patterns in the white dust beneath the poised Spitfires whose elliptical wings offer the only suggestion of elegance in this disagreeable place.

Takali is home for the pilots and ground crews of RAF Squadron 249, the most dishevelled collection of men to be found anywhere in the RAF. Their clothing is disgraceful: the patchwork of various military kits cannot be called uniforms. Their manners are equally graceless.

Even the operational effectiveness of their aircraft, like everything about 249, is questionable. Anyone can see that the planes, like their pilots, are patched and scarred.

For the Maltese people too this is a summer of deprivation, of near starvation, of living with the threat of constant death from the skies above.

Into this weird landscape, fate places one of the war's

most vivid figures, a young Canadian who is to be celebrated as a fighter, a legendary pilot, a hero.

* * *

George Beurling looks like the kid next door, talks with the intonation of a movie tough guy, and shoots faster and straighter than any hero Hollywood could invent. The Knight of Malta wears no badges of rank into battle. His uniform is a Joseph's coat, fittingly appropriate for this strange, gangling youngster who stalks the enemy with Biblical vengeance.

> *The Lord is my light and my*
> *salvation; whom shall I fear?*

To his wingmates he is a contradiction, gentle yet wild, occasionally dreamy. In the business of flying, fighting, and killing, Beurling seems a man possessed.

They marvel at how he sits with no sign of discomfort, waiting in the stifling cockpit of his Spitfire, eager for battle, oblivious to the debilitating heat and the overpowering smell in this tiny capsule, the reek of glycol, cordite, and someone else's urine and vomit from a previous patrol.

His attention to detail is infuriating. Everything is checked and double-checked—the petrol load, the ammunition belts and pans, the ailerons, the rudder.

His eyes miss nothing: the extraordinary china blue eyes that are as startlingly penetrating as those of a wild dog—distant, strange, fathomless.

Everyone agrees he is eccentric and Beurling's habit of constantly poring over his "black book" is proof enough. The book is a record of previous attacks, its pages a jumble of thousands of figures, a secret formula for shooting down airplanes that only this Merlin of Malta can decipher.

His thoughts are only of impending battle. Beurling does not concern himself with the war itself, or Fascism, or Rommel, or the Middle East, and he says so with characteristic bluntness: "I don't know anything about the strategy in Africa."

All his energies are concentrated on the moment, on the preparation for combat. He wears only the silk inner lining of his flight gloves to better feel the pulse of the Spitfire, to manipulate with precision the levers, knobs, and dials, to time the short explosive throb of the ship's guns.

Then it all comes together rolling down the runway: the dust, the din, the drumming of pebbles against the fuselage and wings as the Spitfire shakes itself from a hot sleep under the Mediterranean sun. Like two animals rising from their lair, pilot and machine are one, the beast and the lion tamer entering the ring for another performance.

They work together exquisitely. Beurling's movements are swift and decisive. He is supremely confident, another hallmark of the flying genius.

The left hand leaves the throttle to tinker with the lever that sets mixture and the proper pitch of the propeller. Now the left hand shoots back delicately sensing the trim on the control column. The right hand is poised over the lever that lifts the undercarriage. All the while the eyes absorb information from the dancing dials: oil temperature and pressure, the flow of fuel, air speed... fifty... sixty... seventy... seventy-two. There is no dial as accurate as Beurling's body to tell him when the Spitfire is airborne.

These preliminaries take only eleven seconds.

The right hand jerks the lever to raise the wheels and then retrieves the stick. The left darts forward to another lever to retract the flaps.

There is a deafening symphony of noise and rushing

wind, the prelude to battle. The Spitfire yaws and he adjusts the rudder to keep the plane straight and true. The ailerons flicker in the sun.

He loves these moments. This is good stuff. This is the best stuff. Kipling says about men and war that it is an adventure of fun in the sun. Beurling believes it.

> *Thou shalt not be afraid*
> *for terror by night; nor*
> *for the arrow that flieth*
> *by day.*

This morning Beurling is aboard one of four Spitfires scrambling from Takali. In pairs the planes flash over the harbour at Valletta and roar out to sea, racing to the southeast, climbing towards the sun that is an orange ball in a white sky.

Beurling sees the enemy first—not the reported fifty fighters and bombers which are headed to the island, but two Italian Macchi 202's limping back to Sicily.

There is no hesitation. He pushes the stick forward. Another attack is underway. The unsuspecting Italians continue to drift homeward, unaware that death stalks the sky. Beurling judges the speed and distance as he closes and dips behind the Macchi on the starboard side. The thumb in the silken glove presses the middle of three firing buttons on the stick. One second later the Macchi breaks apart. Now Beurling skids behind the Macchi on the port side and presses the firing button again. The second Italian explodes.

> *The voice of thy thunder*
> *was in the heavens;*
> *lightnings lightened the*
> *world; the earth trembled*
> *and shook.*

Now the patrol sees the armada. It is four against fifty. Suicidal odds. Yet the four Spitfires plunge into the neatly arranged formation. Incredibly the German and Italian fighters and bombers break and flee. The sky is littered with flashing and twisting airplanes. Within seconds the flight formation is scattered, and it is every pilot for himself. The Spitfires hit and run and then race back to Takali. Once more this summer an attack is stopped.

As the searing days grind by Beurling's score mounts. Within six weeks of his arrival on Malta a hungry press begins to feed on his exploits. By the end of July he is a front-page hero.

Beurling poses as the underdog, a Depression kid who learned to fly against impossible odds, a young man who rode the rails across Canada looking for a chance to fly. He is a determined loner in the RAF, the non-conformist shipped to Malta so that RAF officers could be rid of him in England. His deeds are heroic, his pronouncements on life and combat outrageous.

Of the hell that was Malta Beurling says: "These are the best years of my life." The words are poignantly true and a few years later, in trying to recapture the excitement of battle, Beurling died a horrible death, taking with him forever the secret—whatever it was—that made him unique.

ONE

The Word of God

DECEMBER 6, 1921. It was snowing in Verdun, Quebec, the day George Beurling came into the world. He was born at home, a storey-and-a-half wood-frame house on Church Street not far from the banks of the St. Lawrence River. George was the first son and the third of five children of Frederick Beurling and Hetty Florence Gibbs.

Frederick Beurling was born in Sweden but had been brought to the Miramichi Valley in New Brunswick when his father, an engineer, emigrated to Canada at the turn of the century. Grandfather Beurling had landed a job designing pulp mills for a large lumber concern. It was there, too, that the family name "Beurlingk" was changed to "Beurling", apparently for no other reason than it sounded softer and less foreign to the ear.

When Frederick Beurling left the forests of New Brunswick shortly before the First World War he dreamed of a career as an artist but the best he got was a job as a sign painter. He was by all accounts a competent if not gifted illustrator. But as the years passed George's father rose in the ranks of the Claude Neon Company to the position of production supervisor in the Montreal office.

Frederick Beurling was blond, well over six feet tall, an imposing figure whose gold-rimmed spectacles gave him a scholarly air. He was a stern father but not an ungenerous man. He willingly responded to the boy's growing

7

interest in aviation which began to emerge when George was barely seven. The house was always littered with paper gliders and drawings of aircraft. While Frederick Beurling did not entirely approve of George's passion for flying in later years (he felt it was a rather reckless occupation), he nevertheless contributed to his son's piggybank, money which was used to finance purchases of balsa wood, glue, and paint from which George fashioned hundreds of airplanes, a hobby that continued until he was sixteen.

His mother was a loving woman, proud of her two daughters, Gladys and Elsie, and her three sons, George, Richard, and David, whom she presented to the community neatly dressed and scrubbed — a polite brood respectful of their elders. Mrs. Beurling was born in nearby Pointe St. Charles, another Montreal suburb which, like Verdun, was a working-class community. While she was Canadian-born, Hetty Beurling was proud to be able to trace her ancestors to Yorkshire and Somerset in England.

She was a pretty woman with light brown hair and a round face. Hetty played and later taught piano, one of the few entertainments permitted a young lady of the times.

There was, of course, the Church. Hetty Beurling was raised a Presbyterian and it was at a church supper that she met Fred, the aspiring artist. Their courtship revolved around church functions where they soon became a familiar couple. No one in the community was surprised when they married.

Sometime during the First World War, or shortly after it ended, George's father became dissatisfied with Presbyterianism and turned to the Evangelical sect called the Plymouth Brethren and to one of its sternest break-away congregations, the Exclusive Brethren.

Whatever it was that motivated Beurling senior to take up the Brethren's cause is not clear since the family today steadfastly refuse to discuss their private lives and the influences that played a part in the development of their famous member, George.

On the surface the Brethren appeared no more rigid in their beliefs than other fundamentalist denominations: absolute faith in the Bible, in the truth of its history and moral prescriptions. For the Beurlings there was daily Bible study, frequent readings of the Scriptures at home, and unfailing attendance at Sunday worship. Sunday was sacred.

Where the Brethren differed, however, was in their belief that repentance did not entail redemption, that confession was not a guarantee of salvation. Instead, for the Exclusive Brethren, the expression of guilt was but an initiation rite.

For many Christians the question of sin is partly a matter of personal conscience. For the Exclusive Brethren it was a question of denominational *diktat*. Any deviation would result in social as well as religious excommunication. There was only one path, the straight and narrow.

Every Sunday the Beurlings boarded the trolley car in Verdun for the short ride through the maple-lined streets to the Brethren's Bible Hall on City Councillors' Street in Montreal, a disturbing journey for the elder Beurling but a necessary one even though it meant passing the fleshpots of Montreal, a veritable Sodom of the new world.

For any child of the Brethren, and one can only assume for young George as well, a very strong sense of sin developed early in life. For a child brought up in a Brethren household, even though he or she might later experience a lapse of faith, there was no escape from twinges of conscience when confronted with worldly pleasures, no matter how innocent.

In fact we don't know what effect this puritanical straitjacket had on George as he was growing up. We know, however, that he abandoned the Plymouth Brethren about the time he joined the air force. Except to say that his father was stern and demanding, George Beurling never discussed him. "He was a nice character" was all he told a friend years later.

Yet, the knowledge of the Scriptures received from his parents would haunt young Beurling until the day he died. He convinced Israeli secret agents in the last year of his life that it was the prophecies that impelled him to join Israel in its war of independence in 1948.

While many secular pastimes were not allowed in the Beurling household (it took many years before Beurling senior would consent to have a radio in the home), the family was particularly close and spent many happy and leisurely hours together. One of the family's favourite outings was to the farm Grandfather Gibbs cultivated in what was then open countryside at Terrebonne, north of Montreal.

George loved the outdoors and roamed the fields and woods by himself for hours on end. Today's urban sprawl has since gobbled up much of that bucolic countryside; but in the early 1930s deer were plentiful and beaver paddled in a nearby creek, the same creek in which George and his cousin David Murphy took summer swims.

His aunt Dolly Murphy recalls that her nephew was an "energetic and keenly curious boy" with a particular interest in wildlife. Everyone in Verdun remembers him as quite an athlete. Lithe and quick, he developed into an excellent swimmer and a graceful diver, skills which he patiently refined during visits to Verdun's grand swimming pool, the Natatorium. The building still stands, a stolid reminder of Carnegie-style architecture of the 1920s and 30s, an excessive display of brick and tile with its chiselled Latin name. Mussolini would have been impressed.

George Beurling grew up in the Depression, a time that demanded simple entertainments, and Verdun offered more free and accessible diversions than most cities in Canada. The city sits on historic lands between the banks of the St. Lawrence and the Lachine Canal, the very gateway to the North American continent. George found the old portage beside the canal a favourite place to play "cowboys and Indians" with Cousin David, perhaps his closest and only friend. The old boardwalk that ran along the banks of the St. Lawrence was also a favoured haunt, especially in the spring and fall when he went to the river bank to watch the Canada geese swoop down to rest along the shores during their migrations.

Unlike Montreal's fashionable Westmount, Verdun was and remains a bilingual community where the English-speaking kids quickly picked up the language of the street, a French patois known as "joual". George spoke it with ease, the first indication of his facility with languages. Later he studied German on his own, believing that it would give him an added edge in combat if he could understand German pilots when he tuned in to their radio frequency. Just before he died George was learning Italian which, like everything he attempted, he mastered quickly and expertly. Although few people knew it, at the time of his death he had learned a number of operatic arias which he sang with Latin gusto.

This was the same kind of enthusiasm George brought to the hymns his mother taught him to play on her father's old pump organ in the house at Terrebonne. Sometimes, his Aunt Dolly remembers, when a sudden summer thunderstorm forced everyone to retreat indoors to the living room, they passed the time singing hymns. When the sky cleared and the others went outside, George stayed to bang out and sing popular tunes of the day, mimicking Bing Crosby, crooning ditties that surely would have annoyed his father had he been within hearing.

Dolly Murphy was very close to her nephew. She disagreed with Fred Beurling in his attempts to shield George from secular pleasures. Often she turned a blind eye when she found her son David and George reading the comic strips and following the antics of Maggie and Jiggs or the naked Tarzan. Dolly also allowed the pair to sneak off to a Saturday movie, discreetly neglecting to mention the outing to George's father.

All the neighbours knew that the Beurlings were "Bible thumpers". Still, to them, George did not appear to be different from other children. But the Scriptures had marked George. Truth, honour, and virtue, as taught by the Old Testament Prophets, would have a lasting effect on his thinking. And, as the RCAF would learn, so would the Prophets' teachings of revenge and retribution.

Growing Up

THE 1920s was a decade of innovation for aviation in Canada, a time that profoundly influenced young George growing up in Verdun. This was the age of pioneering flights, the age that gave birth to the legends of the Canadian bush pilots, fliers whose names became household words synonymous with daring and adventure and whose exploits were recounted and marvelled at from the backwoods of eastern Canada to the very reaches of the arctic.

The new age of Canadian aviation dawned the year of George's birth, 1921, when two lumbering Junkers F-13's, owned by Imperial Oil, penetrated the inhospitable northlands of western Canada in search of oil. The flight fired the imagination of Canadians who until now had unreasonably come to believe that aircraft were merely machines of war. The memory of the Western Front was still fresh in the minds of a country whose sons had paid with their lives for the price of victory in the First World War.

In 1926 Canadians read of another significant advancement in peacetime aviation. In the Roaring Twenties, the dizzy decade of stock-market speculation in mining and exploration, a flying outfit that nobody had ever heard of called Western Canada Airways began pushing back the frontiers of northern Ontario and Manitoba.

Until then all exploration had been done by lone prospectors in canoes, men whose horizons were limited by the distance they could paddle before winter freeze-up. Now Western Canada Airways was flying twelve months of the year and tripling the prospects of discovery for the same period of time. *

The pilots of the time were yesterday's astronauts hurtling not into space but to the last frontier of a continent. Where youngsters of the 1960s would emulate the feats of John Glenn in makeshift backyard capsules, the kids of the 1920s and 30s aped the likes of "Wop" May and "Punch" Dickins who roamed the skies of the far north. They were daring, brave, and colourful, no one more so than W. J. "Bucky" Buchanan, a quiet Scot who once flew with T. E. Lawrence as his passenger in Arabia when the legendary Englishman was leading his famous Arab revolt.

Buchanan exemplified, perhaps more than anyone, the image of the rugged adventurous pilot who risked life and limb in open-cockpit aircraft. Once he was offered a tip by the flamboyant Canadian millionaire, Harry McLean, following an extremely hazardous flight in a snowstorm. "Bucky" refused the money. "I'm not a taxi-driver, Mr. McLean. I dinna' take tips," he grunted. Then he added, "But a case of whiskey will do."

But none of these fliers created as much of a sensation in Canada — or elsewhere — as the remarkable Charles Lindbergh. Until his epic solo flight across the Atlantic in 1927, aviation was considered to be a risky enterprise that attracted First World War pilots and circus barnstormers. Lindbergh's contribution to aviation was unequalled. Although Alcock and Brown had preceeded him eight

---

* Western Canada Airways was the first of many pioneering Canadian flying companies to capitalize on the times. By the 1940s the company trademark, the Canada Goose, had become a recognizable symbol in world aviation on the tails of Canadian Pacific Airlines' aircraft and later on the jets of CP Airlines.

years earlier, their flight was considered to have been more a matter of luck than skill. Their detractors pointed to the fliers' near-fatal crash in Ireland as proof. What Lindbergh demonstrated beyond a doubt was that, when proper equipment and skilled pilots were used, commercial airlines could cross oceans no matter how vast and make handsome profits at the same time. The seeds of international commercial aviation as we know it today took root as the decade came to a close.

There is no doubt that these events had a great impact on young George Beurling. His interest in flying was first manifested in model-building; he worked not only from blueprints but from the airplanes themselves which he studied at the old Lasalle Airport and, when it closed down, at Cartierville, behind Mount Royal. Ted Hogan, a bush pilot and flying instructor, could not help but notice the eagerness of the quiet lad who haunted the field.

"You think a lot of flying, don't you?" Hogan asked one day.

"Yes, sir," the boy replied, surprising Hogan with a flood of technical questions. The boy was puzzled about the lift and air flow over the wings, about the movements required to do aerobatics, questions that went far beyond the fundamentals of flight.

As it turned out there could not have been a more apt teacher. Hogan was the archetypal pilot, a man consumed with the passion for flight. He looked the part, too. Hogan was never without his leather flying jacket and he actually wore a white silk scarf.

"I'll take you for a flip sometime," Hogan promised young George one day. "Ask your Mom if it's okay."

Years later Beurling said his parents thought he was kidding when he asked their permission. "Sure, George," his mother had said, "sure. You can fly to the moon!"

In the summer of 1930, George Beurling took his first

flight. It lasted only ten minutes but that brief introduction to flying would change his life. He told himself, riding back to Verdun on the streetcar, that "from now on the world will never be the same again".

For the next seven years the hangars at Cartierville became a second home for George. He did all sorts of jobs: moving aircraft in and out of the hangars, pumping gas, cleaning and polishing the airplanes, running errands. By the time he was twelve, George was going up with Hogan and was allowed to man the controls of the plane. Two years later his mentor allowed the youngster to handle take-offs and landings. In 1938, when he was sixteen, the Verdun teenager made his first solo flight in a Curtiss Rambler equipped with skis. He did two circuits and landings in the single-engine, canvas-covered airplane. The big moment was characteristically underplayed: "It was a swell feeling" was all he said in describing the solo flight.

Within a month Beurling attempted his first aerobatics even though he had only accumulated ninety minutes of flying time. The manoeuvre was a flick roll. He pulled the stick back and gave the Rambler full rudder. An instructor saw the incident and threatened to ground Beurling. "What the hell are you trying to do?" he yelled. This was the first but not the last admonition Beurling would get for unorthodox flying.

Shortly after his first solo flight Beurling quit high school. His father was furious. He had hoped that his son would go on to university and earn a degree, an unlikely prospect considering George's marks. He was not one of Verdun High School's more distinguished scholars: he completed grade nine with an average of 57.2 per cent. His performance in grade school was equally unimpressive. The pilot-to-be failed grade five in 1932. That was the year George changed schools three times, a consequence of frequent moves by the Beurling family. In order to find space to accommodate his growing family, Frederick Beurling uprooted the household five times before George was ten.

Modern psychologists might suggest that the frequent moves affected George's performance in school. His teachers, on the other hand, knew the truth: the boy was bored with school, and the classroom was no match for the excitement of his outside interests.

"He was a strangely quiet youngster," says A. L. Larocque, Beurling's grade-eight teacher, "with a one-track mind which led to flying in every way." Aviation was his only friend and his only hobby. Larocque remembers that George frequently played hooky, readily admitting to having skipped classes to spend time at the airport.

In the classroom Larocque found Beurling interested in practical disciplines like geography and meteorology. His pupil often asked Larocque to provide more information on these subjects. What none of his teachers noted in George was a nascent gift for mathematics which would not mature until years later during his air-force career. Beurling was gifted with a computer-swift mind for solving equations, the complex calculations which made him an almost invincible opponent in wartime dogfights.

To teachers and students alike, Beurling appeared to be quiet and aloof. "He arrived at school alone," Larocque says, "had very few friends, generally kept apart from any groups at recess, and avoided team sports."

Few of the many boys who went to school with George ever got to know him. In truth, the young Beurling had only one passion — flying. To help finance his flying lessons he continued to build and sell his expertly fashioned balsa-wood model planes. Despite his disappointment that the boy had abandoned school, Beurling senior did help the aspiring pilot with gifts of cash from his sign-painter's salary to pay for George's flying lessons. The amounts were pathetically small.

Shortly after leaving school George moved out of his parents' home, a move that suggests there was more friction between father and son than George would later admit. He had taken a full-time job assembling radios in the RCA Victor factory in Montreal and had rented a room near the plant, saying that he hoped to save money on streetcar fare. Clearly, living at home rent free, George might have been able to save most of his meagre ten-dollar weekly salary for flying lessons. As it was, after paying room, board, and laundry, he was able to save little money to put towards lessons.

However, in February 1939, his luck changed. He had heard a rumour around the Cartierville field that a small flying outfit north of Toronto was looking for a pilot, someone who would be willing to work for room and board (instead of wages) for the chance to build up flying time.

So off he went from Montreal to Toronto, hopping a freight train like the thousands of other jobless Canadians who were drifting back and forth across the continent in search of work. From Toronto, George hitchhiked north to the small lumbering town of Gravenhurst. There he was met by a pilot, Smith Langley, who was running freight to the goldfields in Rouyn, Quebec.

Beurling flew as Langley's co-pilot, greedily building up time in his logbook. Years later Beurling was reticent in discussing this period in his life, saying only that the job was monotonous. He was more a stevedore than a pilot as his duties included loading and unloading equipment. However, he polished up his navigation skills making the Rouyn run which, at this time of the year, was plagued by sudden blizzards and lengthy snowstorms. His co-pilot's job demanded more than a measure of concentration in picking up landmarks along the way, mile by tedious mile.

The routine life always bored Beurling and the job of hauling freight was wearing thin, perhaps because he was the number-two man in the operation. One day he came across a story in a Toronto newspaper that told of the handful of American pilots who were on their way to China to fly against the invading Japanese. Beurling reasoned that his mounting flying time could qualify him as a fighter pilot. He gave his notice to Langley as the spring break-up came.

Once more he was riding the rods and travelling what he called "tramp class". His destination was San Francisco. The journey across Canada meant twelve days and nights of hopping freight trains and sleeping in hobo jungles beside the tracks.

At Merritt, British Columbia, the young man interrupted his trip to visit an uncle on his mother's side, a doctor who was so impressed with Beurling's enthusiasm that he gave the boy $500, "real" travelling money. In those days this was an enormous amount of cash, a windfall that Beurling decided to put to good use by buying more flying time.

He left Merritt in style. Abandoning the freights, Beurling bought a one-way ticket for Vancouver. As the train pumped westward to the Pacific, Beurling told himself that his new-found wealth would soon permit him to "really make a pilot of [himself]". By that he meant building up time in his logbook, clocking the additional hours he believed would impress the China-recruiters in California.

Whether or not it was realistic to think that a few hundred hours was enough is debatable. There was no question in his mind, however, that he was embarking on a great adventure. Besides, the alternatives for a young man out of work in the Depression were unattractive. The thought of ending up in one of the government's work camps cutting firewood for twenty cents an hour was not part of Beurling's plan for becoming a free spirit.

When he arrived in Vancouver, Beurling headed imme- diately to Sea Island Airport. There he bought fifty hours more flying time from the Len Foggen Flying School. For the next two months, during May and June, Beurling practised aerobatics high over the Georgia Strait and the then-unpopulated Gulf Islands. As June ended he had logged 120 hours of solo flying time and he was broke. It was time to leave for China.

On Dominion Day, 1939, Beurling packed his few belongings and left Vancouver for San Francisco where he hoped to meet the recruiters. If that failed, he told himself, he would sign aboard a China-bound freighter to work his way across the Pacific. The future looked bright.

Aircraftman No. 1267053, RAFVR

BEURLING'S CHINA ADVENTURE ended in the soot-covered freight yards of Seattle, Washington. He had hopped a south-bound freight in Vancouver in the morning, and by nightfall was in the hands of the U.S. immigration authorities, charged with attempting to enter the United States illegally. He was held in custody for nearly two months. Then, late in August, he was escorted, along with a dozen other illegal immigrants, back to the Canadian border where he was given a one-way ticket to Montreal and put aboard a train. The date was September 1, 1939, the day that ended the Great Depression. Germany had invaded Poland.

As the train huffed through the Rockies and rattled across the prairies, Beurling felt certain that his flying skills would soon be urgently needed. He had convinced himself and his travelling companions that the RCAF would certainly "snap him up" when they looked at his logbook. How many people, he asked, were walking around with a pilot's licence? The train wheels seemed to confirm his hopes as they beat out the miles in unison to the words "gonna fly...gonna fly".

Literally within hours of arriving in Montreal, Beurling was on the doorstep of the RCAF recruiter. Incredibly, the air force turned him down. The humiliation of this rejection was to rankle in Beurling's heart for the rest of his life.

21

He would never forgive the RCAF for that initial rejection of him.

There has been some conjecture about the RCAF's reasons for turning the young pilot away. Beurling's own conclusions, typically, tended to be quite fanciful; he was always prone to fancy — especially in the face of a real or imagined slight. Closest to the truth was his feeling that the RCAF sent him away because he lacked what they called a "formal education". The truth is that the RCAF was woefully small, with just 2,000 officers and men to fly a handful of antiquated training aircraft. This meagre force simply couldn't accommodate the many volunteers who rushed to sign up at the start of the war. The few men who were signed on as pilots in the early days were indeed the ones who were university trained.

Lack of education alone was, of course, too mundane a reason for Beurling, who allowed his imagination to compose a more romantic version of his rejection for service. When he had been riding the rods across Canada, he claimed, he had stopped to participate in a light-airplane show in Edmonton in which two of the competitors were RCAF pilots. Beurling won the flying contest, so his story goes and, stepping up to receive his prize, he had said for all to hear, "If that's the best the RCAF can do, it better get some pilots."

So revenge became for George the RCAF's motive — a much more exciting and plausible justification for his anger than lack of education.

Though the story is a good one, we should view it with skepticism, the same view we should take of Beurling's equally good tale that the superior knowledge of aerobatics that won him the competition was gained under the tutelage of the famed First World War German ace, Ernst Udet. Beurling claimed he had met Udet in Portland, Oregon. While it is true that Udet had been in the U.S., performing as a Hollywood stunt pilot, he had already returned to Germany to join the rebuilding of the Luftwaffe at the time Beurling claimed to have studied with him.

That autumn of 1939 was a melancholy one for George and he turned to the only solace his life offered — flying. He spent the next two months working at odd jobs to finance more flying hours at Cartierville airport. In November his spirits rose when the news broke that the Soviet Union had invaded Finland. Rumours around the airfield had it that the Finns were recruiting pilots. At the Finnish Consulate in Montreal he learned that the rumours were true, and an official there, impressed with the number of flying hours in Beurling's log (more than 150 at this time), tentatively agreed to recruit him. He insisted, however, that since Beurling was not yet twenty-one, he would have to obtain his father's permission to sign up. Frederick Beurling refused; he felt that George was too young and the assignment too dangerous — yet another terrible blow for George. "No China. No Finland," Beurling said, "and not even Canada seemed to want a part of me."

It was an unhappy Christmas, that last Yuletide of the 1930s. The new decade arrived with sleet and snow in January. Anyone riding the streetcar out to Cartierville that winter would have seen the most dejected young man in Montreal. He hung around the airport during those first months, trading chores for airplane rides. Quite literally he would do anything to add to his flying time. Spring came slowly and with it new hope. The Montreal newspapers announced that the RAF was now accepting experienced pilots in Britain. The news was enough for Beurling. One day, in May 1940, he packed a small handgrip and walked to the Montreal docks where he found a Swedish ship, the *Valparaiso*, whose skipper was looking for deckhands. Few sailors wanted the job, which was hardly surprising since the ship was loaded with high explosives. This did not deter Beurling, however, who signed on and set sail. The *Valparaiso* proceeded to Halifax where it joined a convoy bound for Glasgow. There were a few "anxious moments", Beurling wrote, near Ireland when the convoy came under submarine attack; it lost seven ships. The *Valparaiso* made it safely to the Clyde and within hours Beurling had presented himself at the nearest RAF recruiting office in Glasgow.

To his delight and utter surprise, and with little formality, the RAF found his qualifications more than acceptable. All he had to do was produce proof of age. In his haste to get to Scotland, Beurling had forgotten to pack his birth certificate. Perhaps nothing was more characteristic of the impetuous youth than his decision to return by convoy to Montreal to get it. The following September, again travelling as a deckhand, he was back in Scotland where he enlisted as Aircraftman 2nd Class, No. 1267053, in the Royal Air Force Volunteer Reserve. His enlistment had ended two years of searching for a way to devote his considerable energies to flying. But he was to discover to his dismay that it would be at least another eight months before he would be alone at the controls of an airplane. He spent the first three months in a manning depot at Hendon, England, waiting to enter an Initial Training Wing, time which he said was unproductively spent peeling potatoes. Finally, in December 1940, Beurling was posted to Devon where he reluctantly bent to the task of studying mathematics, navigation, and meteorology.

By the spring of 1941, after Beurling had successfully completed his course at ITW, he was ordered to the Midlands and No. 5 Elementary Training School. There at last he found himself behind the controls of an aircraft; but it was there, too, that his enthusiasm brought him into what was to be the first of many conflicts with military officialdom. He buzzed the control tower on a bet and immediately upon landing found himself on the carpet. Luckily, although the chief flying instructor threatened to ground him, no further disciplinary action was taken.

Except for this little episode, George felt comfortable at No. 5 ETS. It was, in fact, the first station where the instructors showed any interest in his previous flying experience. A couple of them even allowed Beurling, after a few ritual take-offs and landings, to range over the countryside hedgehopping and performing slow rolls and loops. Naturally he was ecstatic. It had been nearly a year since he had actually piloted an airplane.

By the end of June 1941, he found himself posted at No. 8 Service Flying School at Montrose, Scotland. It was a bucolic setting, perhaps better suited to weekend hikers or British holidaymakers. The airstrip, a swathe of waving grass, lay between the North Sea and the foothills of the Grampian Mountains. The take-off run passed over a brewery at one end of the field where the whiff of hops tantalized the thirsty pilots as they climbed into the sky. The placid mood of the place, however, contrasted sharply with the frantic pace of the training that the pilots had to undergo. They were scheduled to fly around the clock in all sorts of weather. Faced with the task of churning out graduates as quickly as possible, the instructors pushed themselves, their students, and their aircraft to the limit. Crackups on landing and take-off were frequent. A few days after Beurling's arrival, three airplanes collided in mid-air, killing three instructors and two student pilots. And one cloudy night, while one of Beurling's instructors, H. H. C. Holderness, was observing take-offs, he watched a plane disappear into the black murk and explode in a horrendous burst of orange flame. An instructor and student pilot had flown into a nearby hilltop.

Beurling too came very close to death at No. 8. It was on July 2, a week after he had arrived. He was at the controls of a Miles Master, a single low-wing trainer, with Holderness in the instructor's seat. The Master was one of the early molded-plywood aircraft which duplicated in flight many of the characteristics of the more powerful Hurricane fighter. Beurling rolled down the grassy airstrip, lifted over the brewery, and climbed out above a nearby reservoir; suddenly, there was a complete engine failure. Instantly Holderness, a Rhodes Scholar and former Oxford University Air Squadron pilot, a man with fewer hours in his logbook than his student, grabbed the controls of the plane. He picked out a stony field just beyond the town's reservoir, smacking the Miles down hard and fast. The plane was destroyed but Beurling and Holderness walked away.

"I pushed it into the ground harder than I should have," Holderness said years later, "but I was concerned about hitting a stone fence at the end of the field." Beurling, uncharacteristically, kept his mouth shut but the look he gave Holderness said, "I could have done a hell of a lot better." This was the first of Beurling's lucky crashes.

In spite of difficult conditions, the training and flying continued. At No. 8 the students flew every day. They flew formation, cross-country, aerobatics; there was instrument flying, low-level flying, and simulated strafing attacks (without guns) on ground targets.

Beurling was beside himself with joy. Now, for the first time, he thought, all that training was "leading some-where"—even though there was not yet any dogfighting. There was never any doubt in the minds of the instructors that the young Canadian was very good as he wrestled the trainers through the rainy skies of Scotland. On the ground, however, he was constantly in trouble. For exam-ple, Beurling couldn't understand why one of the sergeants insisted on the students' forming up to march between classes. The man was all spit and polish but more to Beurling's annoyance, he was not a pilot in training. The exact words have been obscured by time but the exchange probably went something like this:

"'urry up you louts," the sergeant yelled in his "limey" accent.

"Stick it," the Canadian yelled back.

"Wot! Wot's that?" the startled sergeant said.

There was silence in the ranks and the confrontation ended for the moment.

However, that evening Beurling went along to the man's billet, entered without knocking, and stared him down.

"I'm the guy," he drawled, "who told you to stick it. Wanna step outside?"

The sergeant accepted the challenge. The fight was a one-punch affair. Beurling knocked the man cold.

While the sergeant never filed a formal complaint, rumour reached the CO and he called the Canadian into his office.

"They're just rumours," Beurling pleaded innocently. "I'm told the sergeant walked into a door."

The matter was dropped.

Near the end of his time at Montrose, Beurling progressed to the Hawker Hurricane, the aircraft that only a year before had played such a significant role in the Battle of Britain. The Hurricane was a thoroughbred but not in a class with the Spitfire, and although its days were numbered it was the fastest and hottest aircraft Beurling had yet flown. He spent his last three weeks in Scotland cautiously learning its characteristics, discovering the lightness of the controls in the air, teaching himself to be wary of the plane's tendency to "drop a wing" on landing, a situation that could result in a ground-loop—a sudden and uncontrolled turn after landing. Beurling found many reasons to appreciate the aircraft but he especially liked the Hurricane because it was a single-seater. At last he was flying alone.

During these closing weeks at Montrose he participated in mock dogfights and, most important, in air-to-air gunnery practice. Of all Beurling's skills, the one which would eventually set him apart from his squadron mates was his shooting ability.

In Scotland a foreshadowing of his famed shooting accuracy was evident in his first attack on a target drogue: with one short burst he parted the drogue from the aircraft towing it.

The first week in September marked the end of his pilot-training days, but there was no formal graduation. The student pilots who passed the course simply went out and bought a pair of wings and sergeant's stripes and then picked up their orders to report to an Operational Training Unit. There is nothing to indicate that any of his instructors felt that Beurling was an exceptional pilot. Certainly he was good, but so were many of the others.

The squadron commander noted in Beurling's logbook nothing better than that he would be "useful as a service pilot". In an oblique reference to his fight with the sergeant, the CO cautioned him to "cultivate a sense of responsibility" or, in other words, to begin taking orders without challenging them.

Holderness, on the hand, recalls more positively that he saw "a single-minded determination about him to excel at perfecting his flying skills".

Beurling had been in the RAF for nearly a year. Yet he was irked that he still hadn't seen combat flying and, more important, that he had not yet flown the true champion of the fighter planes, the Spitfire. His chance came immediately after departing Montrose when he was sent to Operational Training Unit No. 57; here at last he found himself in the cockpit of the famous fighter.

The Vickers-Supermarine Spitfire, in the opinion of most air historians, was the best fighter airplane of the Second World War. It was small, only thirty-six feet wingtip to wingtip; it was heavily armed with a combination of cannon and machine guns; it flew effectively at 44,000 feet, had a rapid rate of climb, and was extremely quick and manoeuvrable. Although later fighter aircraft of the war flew faster, farther, and higher, for its day the Spitfire was a pilot's dream and the enemy's nightmare.

Beurling instantly fell in love with the Spitfire, marvelling at its high performance. So for three months at No. 57 OTU he flew as often as he could — night and day, singly, in pairs, in fours, in V-formation, in twelves in line-astern and line-abreast, in level flight, and, when no one was watching, quite self-indulgently, upside down. That too became one of his trademarks. Years later Beurling told the author Leslie Roberts* that the training at OTU was wonderful.

Nevertheless he was eager to move into the next stage, impatient with the formality of routine. Since he possessed a talent for absolute concentration in whatever interested him, Beurling quickly mastered each lesson. He struck acquaintances as being perpetually restless and incapable of relaxation. For Beurling, idle time was wasted time.

Having been brought up with the Exclusive Brethren, Beurling was a non-drinker who, in fact, found booze offensive. For this reason, he avoided pub-crawling with the other pilots. But, more important, he considered

* Leslie Roberts, a Montreal writer and broadcaster, was the first to document Beurling's feats in Malta. He produced *Malta Spitfire* in nineteen days; it was released in February 1943, and three months later, it was a bestseller.

alcohol to be a drug that dulled the senses, a conviction that turned him off tobacco as well. He felt so strongly about this that he abstained from both for his entire life.

His passionate dislike of drink helped set him apart from the other fliers. Although he spoke with affection of his fellow pilots, Beurling, then as later, was reluctant to form close friendships. His training at OTU ended in December 1941, and his flight commander, Ginger Lacey, a famous Battle of Britain pilot, was suitably enough impressed by the ratings the young flier had received from his instructors to recommend Beurling for a commission. Surprisingly, he turned it down. When Lacey asked why, Beurling laconically answered, "I don't feel like an officer." Though Lacey persisted, Beurling was adamant.

In the middle of December, Sergeant-Pilot Beurling was posted to a line squadron, No. 403, which had just moved to North Weald, Essex. This squadron had been the first of thirty-five RCAF squadrons to have been formed overseas. Within days of his arrival, Beurling was in the air, and he flew his first combat mission on Christmas Day. It was an uneventful flight, one which he later called as "exciting as Toronto on Sunday".

Beurling remained with 403 for nearly four months. The squadron spent most of that time shepherding bombers across the English Channel, an impressive operation with sometimes as many as 200 Spitfires growling towards France. A couple of times when Beurling was along, the formations were jumped by German fighters but in all his time with 403 he never managed to get off an effective shot.

By late spring, 403 Squadron became an exclusively Canadian-manned unit, but since Beurling was Royal Air Force, he was transferred to an RAF squadron, No. 41. Before joining his new outfit his flight commander offered once again to recommend him for a commission.

Once again he wasn't interested; in fact, he was downright petulant.

"It's scarcely any time," he said, "since they wouldn't even let me in the ranks because I didn't have enough education to suit them."

When pressed some months later to explain his reluctance, Beurling responded coldly, "Maybe I still had a chip on my shoulder. Let's skip it."

And so, a sergeant-pilot still, Beurling packed his bags and left the flat Essex countryside for his new posting with 41 Squadron in Sussex. Here, Beurling reported sometime later, he got "off on the wrong foot". He felt that the other pilots treated him from the beginning like a "fresh kid".

In fact that is exactly what they did and, of course, it was perfectly normal. In his first assignment, Beurling was given the number-four position in his section, a spot called "tail-end Charlie" reserved for newcomers because it was the most vulnerable position under attack. The loss of a green pilot was preferable to the loss of an experienced one.

Although Beurling informed his flight commander that he had flown combat patrols for the past three months with 403, he reluctantly accepted the "tail-end Charlie" position.

His first two missions were uneventful, but on the third, a sweep over Calais, five Focke-Wulfs jumped the section, separating Beurling from his wingmates. It was an anxious few moments; his Spitfire suffered a number of serious hits that put half his guns out of action. For Beurling, half was enough. He shot one of the F-W's with a short burst, and the airplane exploded in mid-air. Then he limped back to England, expecting to be praised and congratulated for his first kill. * Instead, upon landing, he

* The plane was badly damaged and a pilot with lesser skills might

was pounced on by the other pilots of his section for deliberately breaking formation. Beurling was livid.

Two days later, still assigned to number-four position, he broke from the flight again to pursue a lone F-W 190; later he confirmed it as destroyed. Once again he was angrily set upon by his wingmates who, this time, reported him to the CO. They accused him of breaking formation and endangering the remaining three members of the section.

From that day on in 41 Squadron, Beurling found himself sent to "Coventry", and life became, as he put it, "progressively more stinking". In the mess he was treated like a leper, but, even worse, he found himself "stood down" on sweep after sweep. In a few weeks he had become a more solitary figure than before, trapped in a kind of exile from his wingmates. Dejected and lonely, Beurling's sole outlet was flying, not in his beloved Spitfire but in a small Tiger Moth which the squadron maintained for liaison between nearby fighter strips. He'd take up the little fabric-covered biplane solo and practise stalls and turns over the misty countryside. On land he was miserable.

Although he was allowed to make three more sweeps with 41 Squadron, none was eventful. Frustrated, Beurling began to search for a way to leave the squadron. One day he overheard a pilot bemoaning an order posting him overseas. Because his wife was expecting their first child, the man was reluctant to leave England. To Beurling this was a heaven-sent opportunity.

Seeing his chance to make a break, Beurling asked the squadron commander to make it possible for him to be the man's replacement. There's no doubt 41 Squadron was

---

have abandoned the Spitfire. Beurling, however, coaxed the plane down — his second close call in a crippled aircraft.

glad to see the brooding Canadian leave.

The very next day Beurling was on his way; his destination wasn't yet clear. By nightfall he found himself at a Channel port and three days later boarded a freighter whose holds contained newly crated Spitfires. Shortly, under cover of darkness, the merchantman sailed, escorted by a destroyer and a single corvette. Seven days after leaving England, the tiny convoy reached Gibraltar where Beurling learned where he was destined—the island of Malta.

FOUR

An Island Besieged

Berlin, October 5, 1940. They say the Duce asked the Fuhrer yesterday why he had given up his plan to invade Britain. Hitler swallowed and then dodged an answer by posing a question of his own.

"Why haven't you, Duce, been able to take a little place like Malta?"

The Italians here say Mussolini screwed up his face and said: "Fuhrer, don't forget that Malta is an island too."

William L. Shirer, *Berlin Diary*

THE MALTESE ISLANDS lie at almost the exact centre of the Mediterranean, a location that makes them strategically vital. The main island, Malta, is approximately seventeen miles long and nine miles wide. There are two other inhabitable islands to the north, Gozo and Comino. The small archipelago is completed by the islets of Cominotto and Filfla.

The origins of Malta's native inhabitants are obscure. While scholars agree they came out of the eastern Mediterranean area, the exact area of origin remains a mystery, a mystery heightened by the uniqueness of their polyglot language. Maltese words derive from Latin, French, Italian, and even Arabic. Later, during the war, when a company of Palestinian ambulance drivers was posted to the island, the Maltese discovered they could understand the

Palestinians even though they spoke different tongues. For some members of Malta's learned community, this was seen to be another clue that the Maltese roots grew from one of the Semitic tribes.

Because the islands lie at the crossroads of the Mediterranean, they have been fated for over a thousand years to be ruled by a succession of foreign powers. Throughout Malta's history many invaders dropped anchor in the green waters of its fine harbours, among them Phoenicians, Romans, and Arabs. None of these groups, however, influenced Maltese culture more than the celibate nobles of the Order of St. John of Jerusalem who instilled in the Maltese their deep Catholic roots. In 1800 the British captured the islands from Napoleon and the British presence was maintained until March 1979.

For the British Empire, colonization did not mean the acceptance of the colour or culture of the peoples whose fate rested in its hands. All through Africa, the Middle East, and India, for example, the colonizer's private clubs and social gatherings were exclusive affairs. The majority of Britons held a condescending view of the native populations who came under their rule in the outposts of the Empire.

Britain's interest in Malta was, from the beginning, purely a strategic one, and the islands became the home of the powerful Mediterranean fleet. The Admiralty was justly proud of its holdings, the only fortress between Gibraltar and Suez.

Before the war, the service life on Malta was dull and tedious at best, a life of routine that saw army officers sweating by day on manoeuvres and idling their evenings away in morose messes stuffed with red leather chairs and regimental silver—a monotony broken only on the weekends when they played polo under a burning sun. The best picture of those languid days in pre-war Malta was captured by the acerbic Evelyn Waugh. He described sailing into Valletta's Grand Harbour one afternoon aboard a P&O steamer after a crossing from Alexandria, a voyage which had featured the ship's band rendering tunes from Gilbert and Sullivan while young officers bound for England on leave affected a casual presence on deck, dressed in army shorts, tennis shirts, and cricket blazers.

The dull and dusty garrison duty on Malta ended on June 10, 1940, the day Benito Mussolini finally stopped procrastinating and came into the war on Hitler's side. Within hours of Il Duce's declaration of war, his planes dropped the first of the tens of thousands of bombs that were to fall on the tiny and isolated islands during the battle for the control of the Mediterranean.

As the bombardment increased, the Royal Navy's Mediterranean fleet was forced to abandon Malta for the safer waters at Gibraltar. But it was not until February 1941 that an event took place that would eventually place Malta in mortal peril. One sunny day, a troopship glided into the Libyan port of Tripoli, its decks lined with the smiling faces of German soldiers. The ship carried two units, the Third Reconnaissance and the 39th Antitank battalions of the Wehrmacht, and their commander, a stocky Swabian with blue eyes, who reviewed his troops the following day in front of Government House. They were all smartly turned out in desert khaki and pith helmets.

Arab notables and Italian generals who viewed the parade were suitably impressed. So they should have been. Erwin Rommel had arrived in Africa, and the small force of men was the vanguard of his famed Afrika Korps.

Within two weeks, the Desert Fox launched his first offensive, and for the next eighteen months he ranged across Tripolitania, Cyrenaica, and deep into Egypt. At one point his battered army sat poised 100 miles from Alexandria, ready to lunge towards the Suez Canal and Cairo, where they dreamed of basking in victory in the shadow of the Pyramids. Only a small railway town called El Alamein, the British Eighth Army, and an irascible professional soldier in a black beret named Bernard Law Montgomery stood in their way.

Rommel, as history knows, never did reach the banks of the Nile and his men would not see the belly dancers of Cairo. Yet his presence in Africa would dominate the Middle East theatre for the entire campaign and for many months no one knew for certain whether, in the end, Rommel or Monty would emerge victorious.

It soon became apparent that Rommel's line of supply —Italian merchant ships carrying arms, food, ammunition and, most important, fuel for his Panzers—would have to be attacked and the Axis convoys sunk as they plied between their Italian ports and North Africa. Overnight, Malta became the base for this war of interdiction, a task that fell to the British bomber and torpedo squadrons assigned to Malta's dusty airfields. Ranging far over the Mediterranean, they hunted down and blasted out of the water the merchant ships carrying Rommel's precious supplies and vital gasoline. Without these materials, there could be little doubt about the ultimate result in Africa. In order to avoid a certain and embarrassing defeat, Hitler finally made a move, one he would have preferred not to make. In October 1941, he ordered Field Marshal Kesselring's Luftflotte II from Russia (where the aircraft were sorely needed) to Italy.

Luftflotte II was a massive air armada of 600 front-line aircraft, including the fearsome new F-version of the Messerschmitt 109. Hitler commanded this powerful force to "neutralize" Malta, which was his way of saying that he wanted the islands pounded into stone and rubble.

Far away in England no one knew better than Winston Churchill how perilous Malta's position was. Even though these were some of the darkest days of the war for the Allies, Churchill responded with his usual vigour to this threat. Malta had to be defended to the death if need be. Since the islands were the only catapult from which RAF bombers could operate against Rommel's supply ships, there was no other option. Churchill would risk his best planes that could match the Messerschmitts. But how would he get them there? Because Malta was beyond the Spitfire's flying range from Gibraltar, the closest base to the island, the RAF had to find another solution. There was only one possibility. They would fly the planes from aircraft-carriers. Churchill realized that to mount the operation successfully he would need more flattops than the Royal Navy could muster. So, he turned to President Roosevelt for help. Within days the U.S.S. *Wasp* joined the H.M.S. *Eagle* for the dangerous operation.

The plan involved some terrible risks. In order to bring the aircraft into safe flying range of Malta, the carriers would first have to penetrate the Axis-dominated Mediterranean to a point off the Algerian coast. The pilots assigned to the rescue mission, almost without exception, would be taking off from the heaving deck of an aircraft-carrier for the first time. Then, once they were airborne, there lay ahead of them a flight of 660 miles, all of it through enemy skies. Finally, the pilots would have to display nearly perfect navigation skills in order to find Malta, a faraway dot in a dangerous sea.

In early March 1942, the first Spitfires were put aboard the *Eagle* at Gibraltar. After they were stripped of some of their guns, the Spitfires were rigged with an extra ninety-gallon fuel tank. While the additional gasoline was a measure of safety for the pilots facing the long flight, the heavy tanks added to the perils of take-off.

The first Spitfire off the *Eagle* was piloted by a handsome twenty-one-year-old acting squadron leader named Stan Grant. The lanky yet graceful Gary Cooperesque figure waited impatiently that March day in the stifling cockpit of his Spitfire Mark Vc. The wind had dropped. Until it picked up, the planes could not be safely launched.

Suddenly, the modest young pilot was summoned from his aircraft to the day cabin of the *Eagle*'s captain for a little morale boost.

"How do you feel?" the captain asked.

"All right, sir," Grant replied.

"Oh, well then, would you like a glass of sherry?"

"Yes. Thanks very much."

When the wind increased, Grant climbed back into his airplane and, with a characteristic lack of further fanfare, took off. From March until October 1942, there were 385 Spitfires flown from the carriers to Malta. Only eighteen failed to reach the island. Four were shot down on the way, and the remaining fourteen simply vanished at sea. These remarkable flights, Churchill later acknowledged, tipped the balance in the struggle for the Middle East.

FIVE

Dangerous Flight

GEORGE BEURLING'S JOURNEY to Malta began, as
it did for other Malta-bound pilots, at Gibraltar, the last
safe anchorage for the British in the Mediterranean. Compared with the England Beurling had just left, Gibraltar
was an Eden. Food, especially fresh fruit, was plentiful.
Semi-tropical, the vulnerable outpost basked in warm
breezes from Morocco. In the world of wartime shortages
the sailors and airmen who passed through "Gib" found
an abundance of luxuries; there was plenty of everything,
including perfume and silk stockings.

Beurling stuffed himself with all the fresh foods he
could find. The pilots knew that here was the last decent
food any of them would eat for months. The unrelenting
air attacks on Malta had created a state of siege; supplies of
food and even fresh water had become critically short.

On the evening of Sunday, June 7, 1942, Beurling
boarded the *Eagle* lying at anchor in the shadow of the
Rock. He and the other pilots spent a fitful night sleeping
on blankets in the companionways below the steel flight
deck where, under the cover of night, the *Eagle*'s sailors
were hauling thirty-two Spitfires aboard.

Before sun-up, the *Eagle* was under way. Beurling came
topside late, as the carrier turned into the Alborán Basin,
the narrow neck of water that separates Africa from
Europe. The ship's bow hissed through the languorous

41

morning swell; all about him there was an air of urgency. Accompanied by the sounds of shrilling pipes and the drumming of the white ensign, flight hands mothered the secured aircraft, whose camouflage colours formed a menacing pattern on the stern of the flight deck.

When there was light enough to read the numbers on the fuselages, Beurling and the other pilots wandered through the anchored Spitfires to claim the planes assigned to them. Beurling found his, a new Mark Vc model, bearing the number BR 380.

The scent of fresh camouflage paint betrayed its newness. He immediately circled the plane to check the ailerons, elevators, and rudder, looking for imperfections. Inside the cockpit he fussed with the control column, took a compass reading, double-checked the fuel gauges and the tanks themselves. Everything was letter perfect, understandably so, since this model was the latest in the line of Vickers Spitfires. Powered by the famous Rolls-Royce Merlin engine, the plane offered a maximum speed of 369 m.p.h. at 19,500 feet; it cruised at 272 m.p.h., and was capable of climbing to 20,000 feet in six minutes. This model carried two Hispano 20mm cannons and four Browning .303 machine guns, each with 350 rounds of ammunition. For the long flight that lay ahead, however, the machine guns would be removed to lighten the load for take-off. In the empty ammo wells Beurling and the others would stow their newly issued tropical gear.

By evening, when each pilot was assured all was ready, the men retreated below the decks for a briefing by a Royal Navy carrier pilot on the rudiments of flying airplanes off the deck of an aircraft-carrier. The mood was a jocular one, perhaps the only defence the pilots could muster before making their first take-off at sea the following morning. The navy pilot sent them to bed with the laconic observation that no Spitfire would be allowed to return to

the *Eagle* after take-off in the event of an engine malfunc-
tion. Casually, he pointed out to them (as if they hadn't
already noticed) that none of the Spitfires was equipped
with the arresting gear needed to bring it to a stop after
landing on deck. If there's any trouble, he continued, the
luckless pilot will have a choice—attempt a belly landing
on the sea or bail out near one of the escort ships, and in
either case hope to be picked up. With that discomforting
thought, Beurling bedded down again on the mattress he
had made out of stacked blankets and spent another restless night.

Daybreak found the carrier off Algiers, turning into a
strong, and welcome, thirty m.p.h. wind. One by one the
Spitfires coughed to life and were sent hurtling down the
deck. But Beurling had to wait; his Spitfire was stuffed
with the third flight far back in the pack of planes. Then
the mechanics descended on Beurling's plane, waiting
until the last minute before take-off before attaching the
power-booster cable needed for ignition, an attempt to
conserve a precious few drops of fuel.

Beurling sat poised in the cockpit, more than ready to be
off. Quickly, the plane shuddered to life; the starting cable
was released, and the young Canadian studied the heaving
deck beyond his windscreen. Suddenly, the same carrier
pilot who had briefed them the night before was on Beurling's wing, yelling in his face to confirm that the propeller
was properly set at fine pitch (the setting required to
produce maximum thrust for take-off). As suddenly as he
appeared, the man was gone to check the next aircraft.
Now there was no aircraft in front of Beurling, only the
lone figure of the launching officer who teased him with
the launching flag. As he waited for it to drop, Beurling
held the stick hard against his stomach and pushed the
throttle forward with his left hand. When the Spitfire
began to buck, the flag dropped, and Beurling released the

brake on the control column. The Spitfire shot forward, and the launch officer disappeared in a blur beyond the starboard wing. Gingerly feeling the trim of the aircraft through the stick, Beurling catapulted ahead and quickly reached the end of the deck. At that moment the plane dropped with a horrifying sinking motion and Beurling had to resist the natural impulse to pull the nose up.

Instead, he held it level for speed, flipped the undercarriage switch, and flew straight and steady. With the wind ripping at his face (all pilots took off with the canopy open) he skimmed over the waves, so low that the wash of his propeller roiled the water below. Slowly Beurling closed the canopy and began his ascent, making a left-hand circuit off the carrier where, at 2,000 feet, the Spitfires formed up into four flights in groups of eight.

They climbed through the scattered clouds and aimed at the rising sun. At 16,000 feet, where the air was smooth, they levelled off. Through the broken cloud below, Africa lay brooding and mysterious, Algeria drifted behind, and soon Tunisia appeared in the distance, the air above it shimmering in the furnace heat rising off the land. Here, the flight banked south off Cap Bon for the dash through the Strait of Sicily. There, too, the flight leaders began to strain to pick out the island of Pantelleria, a signpost in the sea that pointed towards their destination. It was a tense flight because of the long passage over open water, and since there was just enough fuel to reach Malta, fuel consumption had to be carefully monitored.

Twenty minutes after they had spotted Pantelleria, they caught sight of Malta dead ahead. As they approached the landing fields, Malta-based Spitfires screened their arrival from the enemy planes that had come to intercept the newcomers. Flying under this protective umbrella, they howled in from the sea and, to a man, safely delivered the desperately needed aircraft.

Beurling found himself stationed at Takali, a dusty airstrip in the middle of the island. The pounding that it had taken from German and Italian bombers was evident to him as he flattened out for his landing. There were so many bomb craters that it seemed as if he were about to touch down on the moon. The new arrivals were unceremoniously hauled out of the Spitfires by sweating mechanics who scrambled over the planes like gnats. Shortly the Spitfires were refuelled and fully armed. Before the day was out many of the planes had been sent out on patrol, so desperately short of planes was the RAF.

After retrieving his personal gear, Beurling and the other sergeant-pilots were driven to billets north of the field, tucked in a cluster of cactus trees. Beurling, his curiosity insatiable, spent the afternoon exploring his new surroundings.

It was an appalling sight. RAF Takali, he discovered, consisted of two dirt runways in the shape of a lop-sided X. The airfield buildings were scattered about in no discernible pattern. The most important of these, the dispersal hut (pilots waited there for the word to scramble) was an eyesore of crumbling stone, corrugated tin, and broken windows. Other equally dilapidated huts made up the rest of the Takali community. These housed the orderly room, the carpenter's shop, the electrician's section, and the guard room. A sick bay was tucked safely away in a nearby quarry.

To Beurling the place had the familiar look and feel of the kind of sprawling hobo jungle that he had known in Depression Canada. In both, newcomers were warily welcomed but, if they didn't upset the routine too much, they could look forward, in time, to acceptance by the old-timers whose mere presence gave the place a special distinction. They were *survivors*, people to be respected on that account alone.

There was a frontier atmosphere to the place that Beurling found exciting and strange. Between the airport at Takali and the sea, tiny villages hugged the landscape. The little square houses reminded Beurling of cubes of caramel, so soft and rich was the texture of their limestone walls. The rest of the island was an undulating moonscape of lunar-white hills and valleys, broken here and there by clumps of gnarled fig trees or by tropical oleanders just beginning to bloom with pink, red, and white flowers. To the north, overlooking the airfield, the ancient walled towns of Rabat and Mdina clung to the top of the rocky pinnacle that rose above the chalky plain. For Beurling this was a strange, new world, a world unimaginably different from the Canada he had known, a world that abruptly plunged into darkness within minutes of sunset. Exhilarated by his new surroundings yet exhausted by the long flight earlier that day, Beurling fell into bed and slept soundly.

That same night, in his room at a centuries' old inn in the heart of Mdina, an RAF officer sat gloomily studying the list of the names of the fliers who had arrived from the *Eagle*. Although the names were unfamiliar to him, P. B. "Laddie" Lucas dutifully pored over the list of replacement pilots. Lucas, a former Fleet Street reporter, was a product of Britain's public-school system. He was a wiry figure whose quick mind matched his energetic movements. When he spoke, Lucas invariably challenged his listener with a provocative thrust of his chin.

"What do you think of this lot?" he asked of the other officers who shared accommodation with him in the large stone house (once the palace of a Maltese baroness).

There was no immediate response from his fellow officers — for good reason. Previously many of the pilots sent out to Malta had been misfits at home. Some of them simply lacked the social graces that the pre-war RAF expected, others were regarded as troublemakers, and there were serious misgivings about the pilot skills of a few. Again Lucas asked for opinions. He was growing impatient.

As one of the flight commanders of 249 Squadron, he was looking for replacements. The other commander, Robert "Buck" McNair, was a Canadian, a handsome Westerner who cut an imposing military figure. He hoped for a regular air-force career when the war ended, and unfortunately was the last person who would be impressed with someone as unorthodox as Beurling.

Word of Beurling's unruly reputation had already filtered to Malta via that unofficial communications network, the service grapevine.

"Beurling's trouble, Laddie," McNair warned Lucas. And another pilot was quick to agree with him. "Right. Nothing official, mind you, but this chap's a loner. Can't be relied on."

"Would he fit into 249?" Lucas asked.

"Might do," the second pilot said. "But it's a risk. He'll either shoot some down or 'buy it'."

"Why?" Lucas snapped back.

"Not much discipline in the air. Tends to get separated from the squadron," the pilot answered. "Very individualistic but he's got flair."

That information could easily have destroyed Beurling's chances of joining 249 Squadron but fortunately it only increased Lucas's curiosity. Not long ago, as a reporter, he had revelled in meeting the odd-balls and eccentric aristocrats who coloured the British sporting scene. He told McNair and the others that he'd sleep on it and then headed for bed.

The June sun was already high in a brilliant blue sky when Lucas arrived at his office (a battered desk in the dispersal hut) the next morning. The new pilots were waiting there to be screened for assignment. After he had taken his seat on a wobbly chair, he ran his finger down the list and called for Sergeant Beurling.

Soon a tall figure filled the frame of the doorway. The man was well over six feet tall and dressed in a short-sleeve shirt that bore no rank or insignia. Powerful legs were planted beneath a pair of baggy shorts, and the man's kneesocks tumbled around his ankles like those of a British footballer.

"Beurling?" Lucas asked.

"Yeh," Beurling replied cautiously.

"Sit down." Lucas studied the young pilot before him. Already slightly sunburned from his one afternoon on the island, Beurling struck Lucas as extremely poised, with a strange, gentle smile and blond hair that looked suspiciously, and un-militarily, long. Beurling's most striking feature, however, was his extraordinary eyes, ice-blue in colour and as penetrating as an eagle's.

"I felt I was in the presence of a very unusual young man," Lucas said years later. "He didn't give a damn for me. A youngster really who was champing at the bit to get to it, to get an airplane and have a go."

Lucas consequently took an immediate and instinctive liking to the young Canadian and, without wasting time, he explained to Beurling that he was aware of his troubles with 41 Squadron but that he could assure him these were a dead issue — providing Beurling didn't repeat his lone-wolf tactics in the air. Beurling promised.

Basing his decision on no more than intuition, Lucas accepted Beurling for his flight, a posting the squadron's commander, Stan Grant, confirmed. Both Lucas and Grant (the flier who had launched the first Malta-bound Spitfire from the *Eagle* back in March) came to regret their decision.

Lucas assigned Beurling to fly with Raoul Daddo-

Langlois. Daddo-Langlois, known as "Daddy Longlegs" by the other pilots, was a proper and straight-laced young man from the Channel Islands. Lucas waited for a week or so before asking Daddo-Langlois how he was getting on with Beurling.

"God Almighty," Langlois replied, "he's quick and he's got the most marvellous eyes but," he added rather ominously, "he's a hell of a chap at being able to keep with us." For Lucas this was a stab in the heart. Beurling had not yet cured himself of the cardinal sin in combat flying — flying on your own. This was strictly forbidden: aircraft always flew in pairs, and each pilot watched the other's tail.

Lucas immediately called for Beurling.

"Do you like it here?" Lucas began, without wasting time.

"Oh," Beurling answered, "it's marvellous. All that flying in England in those wings with three squadrons, always having to stick together, that's not my idea. This is the real thing. You can make it yourself."

The two of them were sitting in the bombed-out dispersal hut. Flies buzzed in and out of the broken windows, and a hot wind whipped up the chalky dust on the runway beyond. It was a good place to talk, and Beurling began to speak candidly of his problems in England. He told Lucas how strongly he despised sticking to formation and he went on to complain about being ostracized by his wingmates.

"It's difficult for me," Beurling continued, "because of what happened in England. I'm a loner. That's my program, and I've got to play it that way."

Lucas exploded.

"You haven't got to play it that way here," he yelled, pounding the table with his fist. "If you stay with this squadron and play it our way you'll be just a guy in the squadron like any one of the other fellows."

Beurling fixed Lucas with those piercing eyes and slowly a gentle grin crossed his face.

Lucas continued: "You've got to stick to the guy that you're flying with. That's why we are alive. You've got absolute trust from me provided you do this. But if you let me down—and make no mistake about this—you're on the next goddam airplane into the Middle East."

Beurling sensed that this was no idle threat and he imagined himself posted to some dinky behind-the-lines squadron operating in Palestine or Egypt.

And so Laddie Lucas, with an understanding that few who knew Beurling would have, realized that banishing the proud young man from yet another line squadron would be for Beurling the ultimate disgrace.

"Well?" Lucas concluded, "Is it my way or not?"

"Boss," Beurling said slowly, "that's good enough for me."

Although Lucas refuses today to accept any credit for Beurling's extraordinary performance, the Englishman may be too modest. Beurling recognized in Lucas the one characteristic which he most admired—professionalism. Lucas was an experienced combat pilot, a man who knew what it was like. Further, while Lucas ruled his flight with an iron hand, there was also, although it seems contradictory, an informal atmosphere about the squadron. Lucas largely ignored formalities; there was more important and serious business at hand.

Within a month of the show-down with Lucas, Beurling had become a legend in Malta.

SIX

Summer at Takali

HE STOOD ALONE in the windless heat beside the runway. No one took much notice: the other pilots were either too tired or too busy. Down by the caves someone was ranging the guns of an aircraft and the sounds of the firing rolled in urgent bursts over the dusty plain. A truck struggled up the hill towards Mdina. The ubiquitous flies moaned in the hot air, desperate in their search for food. Above, the sky was silent, brilliantly white and empty except for the sun hanging there like a plate of hammered brass.

George Beurling waited — a lean, patient figure, perspiration covering his tanned face, soaking his neck, and flattening the shirt against his back. The sweat rolled down his thighs under his baggy khaki shorts, collecting in the rims of his fallen socks. Since the perspiration made the palms of his hands slippery, he shifted the pistol from one hand to the other, drying his palms against his greasy shorts.

Suddenly he saw it move. Ahead, a hint of a puff of dust in the impoverished landscape. He raised the Smith and Wesson .38 and, carefully aiming ahead of the scurrying reptile, fired one shot. It sounded flat — a screen door banging shut on a summer's day. Then he walked to the scaly mess and kicked it with a dusty boot.

One of George Beurling's fellow pilots had been quietly

sitting nearby watching the Canadian stalk the lizards. As
the gunshot echoed across the Takali plain, A. H.
Donaldson lifted himself off his haunches and joined
Beurling in a little gully.

"Get him?" Donaldson asked.

Beurling smiled, replacing the spent cartridge.

"What's it in aid of?"

"Angles," the Canadian said, explaining that he was
"aiming off", the expression used in calculating the angle
for a deflection shot.

"It sounds complicated," Beurling continued, "but
there isn't really much to it. In laying off the deflection, it's
calculation more than judgment."

It had been two months and more since his heart-
to-heart talk with Laddie Lucas.

As the weeks passed and Beurling's score mounted, his
fellow pilots understandably grew eager to know what
made this strange man so deadly effective. It baffled them
that the gangly, shuffling, and seemingly awkward figure
they saw on the ground had become so beautifully coor-
dinated in the air.

"After seeing the enemy plane and getting into position," Lucas explains, "there was this business of going
straight in as hard as he could go. And WUMP! and away. It
was the cleanness of the kill: he was in close, a short burst
and away. And yet here was this guy on the ground, hair
all over the place, untidy, and so on. It was the most
extraordinary transformation."

Of course there were many reasons for Beurling's suc-
cesses in the air. One was his remarkable eyesight. While
his records list him as having only 20/20 vision, everyone
who ever flew with him knew he possessed "super vision". Of all the stories about him told by his wingmates,
most concern his extraordinary vision. The story most
repeated involved Beurling waiting around the dispersal

hut at Kenley in England one day when he suddenly announced, "Here come the Forts." No one else could hear them let alone see them. "There are thirty-six," he said. Moments later the others heard the Flying Fortresses, and shortly the big planes began appearing in the far distance. Everyone started counting. There were thirty-six.

In combat in Malta Beurling *always* spotted the enemy in the air before anyone else. His wingmates marvelled at his gift, one for which there was no scientific explanation.

To improve his already incredible vision, Beurling devised an exercise to refine his focusing powers. He would train his eyes on an object, perhaps three feet away, then suddenly lift them to the very farthest horizon, trying to reduce to a microsecond the time needed to adjust his focus.

His vision did not diminish following the war either. Once, walking with a friend down the street, he casually remarked, "See that girl across the street. She's got blue eyes." Of course the woman was too far away for the friend to tell. So they crossed the street and passed the girl. Her eyes were blue.

At the height of Beurling's fame in Malta his "super vision" gave him an obvious advantage — the element of surprise. Four or five seconds doesn't sound like much of an edge but those critical seconds allowed him time to begin his deadly moves.

But while many pilots possessed keen eyesight few could match Beurling's shooting skill. This was his greatest mark of distinction. Beurling refuted any suggestion that it was a natural ability, insisting that it was an acquired skill, one which he pursued with dogged determination. The lonely forays around the dusty environs of Takali in search of lizards was a perfect example of his almost mystical dedication to the science of killing.

In combat flying there are essentially only three shooting angles. The simplest but most dangerous of these is to fly at an enemy head on. The problem with this angle is that there is a frighteningly high likelihood of collision when aircraft are closing at a combined speed of more than 600 m.p.h.

The pilots knew that the safest and easiest position for attack was at the same altitude as the prey and directly behind him. The perfect shot, however, was rare. To achieve it a pilot had to position himself undetected; in combat in Malta this seldom was possible since the RAF was outnumbered by at least ten to one. Survival depended on how quickly the Spitfire pilots could get the first shot away after spotting an enemy fighter. Inevitably this meant firing at an angle, by far the most difficult calculation.

Beurling became the best in the world at this kind of shooting. The air force called it "deflection shooting".

To make a deflection shot a pilot must first determine the speed of the enemy aircraft. He must also determine the point ahead of the enemy where his own bullets will meet the enemy plane. Estimating the angle of attack and the speed of the enemy fighter required such an awesome range of calculations that some fighter pilots found themselves incapable of deflection shooting.

The simple, almost primitive gunsight used in the Spitfires at the time made deflection shooting even more difficult. The sight was no more than a three-inch circle on a piece of clear plastic with a dot in the centre of the circle. It was up to the pilot to calculate how to score a hit. A direct attack from the rear was easy, of course, because the pilot simply centred the dot on the enemy aircraft. But, as the angle of attack increased, the pilot's calculations became more complex. In a matter of microseconds he had to determine his enemy's speed and angle in relation to his own; and then, having worked that out, he had to aim his own aircraft with only the aid of the circle and dot on the plexiglass. No pilot on Malta could match Beurling's skill in this manoeuvre.

To hone his skill, Beurling took up lizard hunting around the Takali airport on the days when he was not flying. The island abounded with lizards; the most common variety was about five inches in length. Dressed like a big-game hunter, in shorts and khaki shirt, Beurling would stand motionless in the burning sun waiting for his victims. To complicate the hunt, he would shoot only at lizards a certain distance away, the distance at which he judged the lizard was relative in size to that of a Messerschmitt or an Italian Macchi fighter at 300 yards.*

Some of Beurling's squadron mates felt his shooting forays were mere exhibitionism. Perhaps too they felt guilty since most of them were quite content to drink and unwind that way on the days when they did not have to fly.

As soon as Beurling arrived on Malta, he began recording the details of each of his successful attacks and each of his misses in a black book. He then designed a set of formulae and a graph that took into account the thousands of pieces of information he had compiled. The formulae and the graphs were then committed to memory so that, when the occasion arose, he could draw on this information in a split second, an Olympian feat of mental gymnastics that could have been performed only by a brilliant natural mathematician.

Beurling did not hoard his formulae; they were available to any comrade who asked. One day, for instance, he spent an hour trying to explain them to Stan Grant, the

* It was a rule of thumb for fighter pilots that any target farther away than 300 yards was a longshot. Beurling preferred 250 yards. For him that was a sure kill.

squadron commander of 249. But Grant later had to admit there were so many figures that it was impossible for him to commit the formulae to memory.

On July 1, 1942, barely a month after George Beurling had arrived on Malta, General Rommel launched his first attack against El Alamein. The battle raged for twenty-six days, and its outcome greatly depended on how successfully the rapacious German panzers could be kept supplied from the Italian mainland. Not surprisingly, the pattern of combat devised to prevent Rommel from receiving his materiel became predictable. The RAF bomber squadrons on Malta would seek out the enemy merchant ships bound for Africa; the Italian and German air forces, operating from their bases in Sicily, would attempt to obliterate the RAF bomber bases on Malta, and the beefed-up Malta Spitfire squadrons would try to intercept the enemy planes before they could reach the island. The bedlam that resulted was just as predictable. For the month of July the clamour of battle rent the skies above Malta, an epic din which saw George Beurling emerge, no longer an exile in his own ranks but a front-page hero and a contemporary Knight of Malta.

British tactics for the defence of Malta were deceptively simple. The heart of the defence lay in a musty war room buried deep in the heart of the island. The operations room of RAF Headquarters, called the "great ditch", had been carved out of the soft limestone near the harbour at Valletta, the capital. There, the senior controller, himself a fighter pilot, waited for the first reports of radar sightings of approaching enemy planes. At Takali, or the other main fighter fields at Luqa and Halfar, the Spitfire pilots waited at the dispersal huts. As soon as enemy planes were picked up by radar, the word was flashed to the squadrons, and in a minute the Spitfires were airborne, clawing their way skyward to gain altitude in the shortest time possible. It was a frantic sixty seconds. As the pilots wrestled the groaning fighters down the runway—dodging rocks, bomb craters, and swirling dust—they had to absorb the vital information crackling in their radios about the position, altitude, and speed of the advancing enemy. If the warning came early enough, the Spitfires were able to set themselves up south of the islands—the most advantageous position for an attack. There the sun was behind them, and it was the incoming German and Italian pilots who were forced to stare into the blinding Mediterranean sky. Although attacking out of the sun was a fundamental technique for any fighter pilot, the British had introduced a more important tactic—a simple formation that the Spitfire pilots employed—which, in the last analysis, turned the tide of battle.

The Spitfires flew in pairs, never, absolutely never, singly. The two-plane formation was a refinement of the "Finger Four", a formation invented by the Germans, and successfully tested by them in the Spanish Civil War. The RAF adopted the pattern early in the war, and a fearsome Canadian pilot, Stan Turner, introduced it to Malta in the early days of air combat over the island, long before Beurling had arrived.

The formation was as simple as it was effective. Two pilots flew side by side in level flight, each disregarding the "blind spot" behind him. Instead, each looked inward towards the other. That way they focused on one another's respective "blind spot" and eliminated the chances of being surprised by an enemy fighter. It meant that instead of each pilot trying to cover 360 degrees of sky with his eyes he was only responsible for 180 degrees.* Or, to put it another way, the pilot on the right ignored the

* Although the Spitfires were equipped with mirrors mounted outside the cockpit canopy, most pilots found them useless because of their size and the distortion created by air turbulence in flight.

sky to his right and rear, and concentrated on the front and left. The pilot on the left reversed the process. As a team they covered the sky completely. Thus, if both pilots remained alert, it was virtually impossible for a marauding enemy fighter to surprise them. After the show-down with Lucas, Beurling recognized the effectiveness of the formation and followed its demands to the letter.

After nearly a month on the island, Beurling had flown six patrols. Of these only one was eventful: he and another pilot ran into four Messerschmitts and, in a brief mêlée, Beurling blew the tail off one of the German planes with a single burst from his guns. However, since no one saw it crash, he was credited with only damaging the Messerschmitt.

On July 6, however, Beurling's score took a dramatic turn. He was aboard one of eight Spitfires that were scrambled to intercept three Italian Cant bombers and thirty Macchi 202's, Italy's top-line fighter. The eight Spitfires, finding themselves sitting on top of the incoming formation at 22,000 feet, dived straight into the Italians. In seconds, with one burst Beurling had damaged a bomber. Then, suddenly he was on the tail of a Macchi whose pilot, spotting the Spitfire, plunged into a dive. The Canadian chased his prey for 15,000 feet and, when the Italian pulled up at 5,000 feet, Beurling let go a two-second burst from 300 yards away. It was a perfect hit.

Although he wasn't aware that he had been fired on, when Beurling inspected his Spitfire back at Takali, he found it riddled with bullets. Undaunted, he took off at noon in another Spitfire for a second patrol but this time he wasn't able to locate the enemy. That evening, however, just before dusk, he was in the air again in a patrol of four Spitfires. Radar had shown two German JU88's and twenty Messerschmitts, the deadly 109F's, heading towards Malta. There they were in the failing light. After the four Spitfires dived and split up the formation, Beurling spotted one of the fighters breaking away on its own.

He followed closely while the fleeing pilot tried to escape at low level over the sea. And then, judging the moment right, he laid down a two-second burst and the German crashed into the Mediterranean.

On that day alone, Beurling's total was four: one Messerschmitt and two Macchi fighters destroyed and one Cant bomber damaged. It was only the beginning of his days of glory; there would be more such days in the weeks ahead.

As those hot July days passed, Beurling was called on again and again to make his deadly calculations. Each day saw wave after wave of German and Italian planes hurtling towards Malta to bomb and strafe Takali and the other RAF fields.

Day after day the Spitfires scrambled to intercept the enemy, whom Beurling began calling "those goddam screwballs". This became his constant cry, and it earned him the nickname "screwball".* Although this unfortunate name was not a reflection on his skill or personality, it stuck and later it created in the public's mind the image of a wild and reckless figure. Beurling was anything but reckless. Indeed, his decisiveness in combat had won him quiet respect from his wingmates. And, further, his aloof but purposeful behaviour on the ground ignited a growing admiration for the single-minded young man. In fact, most of his wingmates grew to enjoy him for his eccentricities, his daily ritual of poring over the contents of

---

* Later the name was dropped—it seemed inappropriate that the country's greatest hero should be called "screwball"—and suddenly the press began referring to him as "Buzz". David Beurling says the family is not even sure how the second nickname originated. Beurling's few friends never used either nickname; they called him George.

his black book and his lonely lizard safaris around Takali.

Beurling may have reasoned that these eccentric pastimes were an essential diversion from the bedlam of Malta. Some pilots sought relief from more obvious entertainments. There were drinking sessions that would last long into the night, or for as long as the supply of alcohol held out. There was one brewery on the island, Farsons, but its production depended on how rapidly it could make repairs after numerous bombing raids. Beurling excluded himself from these drinking bouts. His recreation consisted of occasional swims with another pilot, Joseph Paradis, a French Canadian from Shawinigan Falls, Quebec. After Paradis was killed the third week in July, Beurling went out of his way not to form another close friendship.

"I have made it a rule not to make close friends," he said. "If a fellow has had a dear friend shot down it might interfere with his mental calculations in the air." It was not just the loss of Paradis that triggered this decision, but Beurling's awareness of the constant attrition of men. In just one week in July, for instance, 249 Squadron lost half its pilots in dogfights.

Yet while he kept to himself on the ground, Beurling was always willing to volunteer for flying.

"All through the worst times," Lucas recalls, "I never saw Beurling turn down a chance to fly. Not once did he slump back. Never." And Stan Grant even grew to suspect that the Canadian arranged privately with other pilots to replace them on combat patrols when the strain began to wear away at their resolve.

Of course, the strain was not limited to the pilots. The Maltese civilians also suffered terribly. Before the war there had been a so-called "Italian element" in Malta society which favoured closer ties with Italy. This element was led by a newspaperman named Enrico Mizzi. When war broke out, Mizzi was whisked out of Malta and interned in Uganda, a decision that hardly endeared the Britons to his followers. As a result of the bad feeling, on those rare times that a 249 pilot got a day off in Valletta he was likely to be sneered at. In addition, disgruntled Maltese civilians would call out the single word "pee-lot" in a disparaging way.

The RAF had enlisted Maltese civilians to help repair the constantly damaged Takali strip and to keep intact the sandbag revetments which surrounded the precious Spitfires. This important task was performed as well by both officers and enlisted men. Unhappily, when the air-raid sirens wailed the civilian workers were often the first to head to the slit trenches beside the runway. Their rush to shelter infuriated the pilots who felt that protecting the aircraft from shrapnel was more important than personal safety.

Of course, not every Maltese acted in this fashion. In fact, in spite of the horrible suffering from bombs and scarcities, and the heavy toll of casualties (mounting to 1 in 160), most Maltese acted with such courage and determination that in 1942 King George VI bestowed on the island the George Cross, Britain's highest decoration for civilian gallantry.

Beurling's own bravery, too, quickly came to be recognized by the RAF. In the middle of July he was awarded the Distinguished Flying Medal for his action in the patrols of July 6. But with that honour came a recommendation from Laddie Lucas that it was now time for Beurling to accept a commission. Once again Beurling declined.

Soon Stan Grant was on the case, and one morning the young Canadian appeared in the squadron leader's office, a dusty, windowless stone hut at Takali. With typical unconcern for ceremony, Beurling leaned against the wall, his hands stuffed into the pockets of his shorts.

"Are you interested in a commission?" Grant asked.

"No," Beurling said, a response so startlingly short and definitive that it seemed futile to Grant to pursue the issue.

"You may leave," Grant shot back just as curtly. Everyone's nerves were taut, including Grant's. The very correct squadron leader, barely a year older than Beurling, had just taken over as station commander at Takali. Later he would leave for a stint "down the hole" in Valletta as a fighter controller, an assignment with awesome responsibilities; the outcome of a scramble hinged on the controller's skill in directing the Spitfires to a successful intercept.

It was a job made even more difficult during July because of seriously dwindling gasoline supplies; only two ships had been able to get through to Malta since March and every ounce of food and petrol had become precious. Just as critical for civilians was the rationing of food. In fact, the situation became so desperate that the Maltese began to fear starvation. For the RAF pilots and ground crews life was scarcely better. They survived on a diet of bully beef that was served baked, boiled, or fried.

"A filthy, greasy mess," Lucas concurs. "It was an awful life, to be honest." His memory of those horrible conditions remains vivid more than three decades later. "Nothing," he says, "would induce me to go back to Malta for a holiday."

The rotting rations inflicted on the pilots a painful and debilitating form of dysentery which they called "Malta Dog". For some inexplicable reason the Dog struck every fortnight with almost predictable regularity, leaving its victims completely, often instantly, incapacitated. In some cases, airborne pilots could not avoid fouling their Spitfire cockpits during a sudden attack of the Dog.

To add to the misery, many pilots developed skin infections owing to the scarcity of vegetables. On Beurling's face and neck boils erupted which quickly became infected because of the constant rubbing of his flying helmet and oxygen mask. Further, many pilots were stricken with sandfly fever, an illness that left them with blinding headaches for weeks on end.

The Axis blockade on the supply convoys created yet another hardship, a scarcity of clothing. Since replacement pilots arrived from the carriers with not much more than a hobo's change of clothes stowed in empty ammo wells, dress quickly became informal, even downright colourful. An American pilot, Reade Tilley, took to wearing a pair of white DAKS slacks and the only jacket at hand, a brown number which he stuffed into a dye vat hoping to change it to air-force blue. It came out purple. Beurling himself customarily wore a dark blue Royal Australian Air Force jacket with his stained, dirty shorts.

The casual informality went well beyond clothes. There were no parades, no bugles sounding evening "Retreat", and very little saluting, least of all from Beurling who instead persisted in addressing Lucas and Grant as "boss". The squadron dropped other military trappings as well. Since there was no time to paint the squadron's official letters of designation, GN, on replacement Spitfires, the ground crew slapped on a hastily painted T for "Tiger Squadron", the name used for local radio identification. And after 249's depleted ranks came to be filled by Australians, New Zealanders, Rhodesians, South Africans, Canadians and, like a page from the script of a wartime movie, an American from Texas, the squadron lost its British identity as well as its military look. And yet, though un-British, informal, un-military, a casual patchwork of nationalities, 249 continued to do its job and to do it effectively.

It goes without saying, of course, that Beurling loved the informality. It's hard to imagine him performing so well without it. Those days and months on Malta were special to him. Long after he left combat he said, "I'd give ten years of my life to live those days over again."

*   *   *

While life at Takali meant heat, fatigue, hunger, and disorganization, enemy pilots faced the same hardships and deprivations.

July 27, 1942, was a typical day for an Italian pilot, twenty-five-year-old Faliero Gelli. He was stationed at Gela, an airfield situated in the Sicilian toe, just sixty miles from Malta. Like his RAF enemies, he was up early that morning — 4:30. As he sat munching a piece of stale black bread between sips of coffee, his mood shifted between gloom and hope. His bags were packed for a leave home to Pistoia, near Florence, where his family and his girlfriend eagerly awaited his arrival. The night before, his furlough had been postponed by one day. A new lieutenant (who had never flown in combat) had just been assigned to the squadron and Gelli's commander wanted the man to fly his first mission with an experienced pilot. Gelli was that pilot. He had been in the Italian air force since 1936; like Beurling he was a sergeant-pilot but with two kills to his record. He was unhappy with the assignment despite the ringing words of Il Duce who had visited the airfield only the day before to bestow on him the Italian Bronze Cross. Mussolini had exhorted him, and his fellow medal recipients, to greater feats over Malta. In truth, Gelli wanted to go home to see his girl.

Gelli finished his meagre breakfast and wandered to the flight line to claim his Macchi 202, and to meet the new officer — a young man, Gelli remembers, flushed with excitement as he prepared for his first combat mission. They finally got under way at 11 a.m.; they took off from Gela, Sicily, as part of a major attack being mounted that morning involving Junkers, Messerschmitts, and Macchis. Gelli and the new pilot headed one flight in the formation of fifty aircraft. Solace in numbers, the Italian thought. As they approached Malta, Gelli discovered that his new wingman had disappeared. Green fool, Gelli said to himself, just as he experienced a new but immediately recognizable sensation. His fighter was rocking violently. Bits of wing were flying everywhere and black smoke poured from the engine cowling. He was at 25,000 feet. Immediately he pushed the aircraft into a dive. Down he went, feverishly trying to maintain control.

When he pulled from the dive he found himself over Gozo, the second largest island north of Malta. He was directly over Victoria, its capital, so low now that the top of a church steeple loomed above his port wing. Seconds later he pancaked into a rocky field just outside the town. The impact of the crash was so severe that the bolts holding his cockpit seat were sheared off, throwing Gelli forward against the instrument panel and knocking him unconscious.

The Maltese who pulled him free of the aircraft were startled by the condition of the fallen Italian fighter pilot. His head had ballooned to twice normal size. Hours later he found himself in a hospital on Malta where, standing before his bed, was a lean, fair-haired RAF interrogator who was asking, in perfect Italian, whether Gelli would like to meet the man who had shot him down.

"Of course," Gelli replied gallantly.

"His name is Beurling," the Britisher said, "and, like you, he is a sergeant-pilot."

The fateful meeting would not take place. Only days before Lucas had visited the crew of an enemy bomber which he had brought down. The sight of the wounded crew so disturbed him that he ordered that no such visits be permitted, although previously it had been the usual practice.

"When I approached one of the beds, a chap held up the stump of his arm," Lucas recalled years later. "It just simply made me feel absolutely sick and I never let any pilots go anywhere near these fellows after that."

Although Gelli never met Beurling, he is a unique human statistic: the only man who survived an attack by the Canadian ace. Further, he is able to confirm Beurling's great skill at surprising his opponents. Gelli didn't know what hit him.

*　　*　　*

July 27 had been a memorable day for Beurling. After dispatching Gelli he destroyed another Macchi and a Messerschmitt. He also damaged a second Me-109. Then the Spitfire patrol screamed back to Takali to reload but, after finding the airstrip full of bomb holes, Beurling put down at nearby Luqa. Gassed and re-armed he was soon in the air again, this time to take on twenty Messerschmitts. The clash occurred at 17,000 feet. There, Beurling, moving like some cattle wrangler from the west, herded two Me's out of the pack, drove them down to 1,000 feet, and dispatched both into the green Mediterranean. Within two days he had shot down yet another Messerschmitt, so that now, after barely two months on Malta, his score had climbed to twenty-one: sixteen enemy planes destroyed, one probably destroyed, and four damaged.

In Africa, during the same month, Rommel's score was less impressive. By the end of July, his drive to overrun El Alamein had collapsed, and Axis convoys from Sicily to Africa had started to peter off. This brief lull came none too soon for both the Maltese and the pilots. It came mercifully too for George Beurling; the strain of combat in July started to have its effects on the youngster from Verdun.

He was losing weight rapidly, dropping from 175

pounds to 140. Weakened by the tension of battle and the lack of a proper diet, he collapsed with a severe case of the Dog, an attack that left him barely able to walk. As he lay in his bunk in the sergeants' billets, a signal from London ordered him to accept, finally, the officer's commission he had so many times rejected. Too weak to protest, he received the honour in silence. At home, however, the praise for the young Canadian was loud and his feats of daring commanded front-page news stories.

As a pilot-officer, Beurling moved from the cactus groves and the dusty bombcraters to the hilltop town of Mdina, high above the plain of Takali. The officers' mess was located in a charming, twenty-three-room house with cool vaulted ceilings, a small palace that had been the home of the Baroness Xara. Its terrace offered spectacular views of the island: immediately below lay the airfield; to the northwest, St. Paul's Bay simmered in the sun, a resort in more peaceful times. There, legend said, St. Paul had been shipwrecked in 60 A.D. To the south, Valletta perched on the horizon, a few buildings left standing.

Beurling and his fellow officers found the back terrace of the palace a perfect observation platform from which to watch enemy planes bombing and strafing the airfield. The attackers flew in so low that an observer on the terrace could actually look down on incoming aircraft and clearly see the faces of the Germans and Italians.

Beurling's first week at the Xara Palace was spent in bed. A week was long enough for much of his strength to return. Beurling then went back to duty. The routine never varied, and the residents of Mdina knew it as well as the pilots. Each morning, long before it was light, the sound of the fliers' shuffling feet echoed across the cobblestones of the tiny courtyard in front of the palace. Then, an old bus coughed to life and, groaning into low gear, made its way down the steep road to the airfield.

Inside the bus Beurling and the others would sit bundled in heavy sweaters against the early morning chill. The pilots found it maddening how quickly temperatures rose once the sun was up. It was a short bus ride, just five minutes to the airfield and the dispersal hut where they breakfasted on the unspeakably greasy bully beef, washed down with cups of tea. Beurling, who was constantly hungry, forced himself to slop up the stuff with chunks of Maltese bread even though he knew it would soon have him hovering over the nearest latrine.

While they waited for the word to scramble, the men developed their own ways of passing the time. Some wrote letters, others played poker; George, like some gaunt actuary from a Dickens novel, busied himself entering deflection figures in his black, dog-eared notebook. More often than not he waited in the cockpit of the Spitfire assigned to him that day. *

But whatever plane was his on a given day, it got a thorough going-over by the blond ace. He paid particular attention to his ammunition loads, and he frequently challenged the RAF armourers if he found the slightest imperfection in the way they had belted the bullets. Because he found that belts jammed frequently, he preferred pans of ammo when he could get them.

Another problem that bothered Beurling was tracer bullets. The bright flash of their trajectories threw his aim off instead of helping it. Their mesmerizing effect upset his concentration and caused him to miss the first telltale signs of a hit, the bits of debris and puffs of smoke. Also,

* Since it was rare for all twelve airplanes of the squadron to be operational, it was impossible for a pilot to claim the same aircraft two days in a row. Though there was on Malta no "Beurling Spitfire" — the personal aircraft the Canadian would have enjoyed had he flown in Britain — the log of 249 Squadron does show that Beurling flew most often a Spitfire Mark Vc marked TZ BR 135.

he preferred that his cannon and machine guns be har-
monized to throw their greatest firepower 250 yards ahead
of the plane (50 yards less than the more usual 300 yards).
He went to great trouble to align his guns for this distance,
but often on patrol he was forced to fly an aircraft whose
weapons had been set to the 300-yard standard. There
wasn't always time to adjust the guns before a scramble.

To his fellow pilots, the Canadian appeared obsessive
about detail, and they felt that he was especially picky
about his aircraft's guns and ammunition.

All war-movie buffs have memories of celluloid heroes
on the tail of an enemy aircraft, peppering away with
machine guns for what seemed like hours. In fact, the
actual machine guns, four Browning .303's, and two
20mm cannon carried enough ammunition to fire for only
thirteen seconds, enough time, by Beurling's calculations,
for seven shots or seven bursts lasting just under two
seconds each. Beurling was determined to use those thirteen seconds to the best possible effect. If this meant
chewing out the ground crew about sloppily belted ammo
loads, too bad.

Beurling's airmanship was as impressive as his shooting. Much has been written about certain persons who
display natural ability at the controls of an airplane. The
late Frank Tallman, a former U.S. Navy flight instructor
and later a famous Hollywood stunt pilot, didn't believe
that there was such a thing as a natural pilot. He said that
those who appeared to be "naturals" were simply indi-
viduals who possessed more energy, drive, and desire than
the average. Always confident and graceful, George
Beurling was a "natural" in Tallman's sense of the word.
Beurling kept his combat manoeuvres to a minimum,
using mainly the steep turn, the slide slip, or the barrel roll.
His most effective evasive tactic was what he called "an
aileron turn where you kick everything [the stick and the

rudder] into the corner". This movement flips the aircraft over and causes it to drop like a rock.

In spite of all his skills in handling aircraft, Beurling did make a few mistakes. On August 8, a German pilot got a shot on Beurling's Spitfire (not surprisingly since the patrol of four Spitfires was up against twenty Me-109's). The shot cut the Canadian's engine power by half. He barely made it back to Malta where he crash-landed in a field, knocking himself out. When he came to he hitch-hiked back to Takali. It was the third crash that we know about and another from which he walked away.

For Beurling the rest of August was unproductive. In between bouts of the Dog he took part in a new offensive against German and Italian air bases in Sicily. August, too, saw the dramatic arrival of a battered convoy that was the result of a do-or-die operation called "Pedestal". In order to relieve the desperate supply situation at Malta, the Royal Navy had mounted a fleet of fifty-nine warships to shepherd fourteen merchant ships carrying airplane fuel, food, and ammunition. Although Pedestal was successful, its costs were high: only five of the supply vessels managed to reach Valletta's harbour, including the crippled tanker *Ohio*. The siege of Malta was broken but it would be another two months before it would end and Rommel would embark on his long retreat.

To celebrate the convoy's arrival, Beurling and other Spitfire pilots escorted the limping merchantmen into port. Beurling could not resist showing off. He marked the arrival of the *Ohio* by flying a few feet above Valletta's main street upside down.

In September, the RAF stepped-up its offensive against the enemy bases in Sicily. Still the Messerschmitts and Macchis counterattacked fiercely. In addition to the Sicilian sweeps, hectic scrambles continued. All the while the Dog continued to plague Beurling and under the strain of combat patrols, his general health deteriorated rapidly. The young Beurling had come to the island in robust health, but now he was skeletal and gaunt, weighing no more than 125 pounds. He insisted on flying and haunted the dispersal hut day in and day out. He seemed to be everywhere, hair all over the place, eyes glinting with excitement. He was a frightening sight. Many of the pilots from June and July were gone now, killed, wounded, or posted home. His favourite, Laddie Lucas, had left, too.

It was about that time that air combat began to take on a new and ugly dimension. One day, during what was otherwise a normal scramble, a Rhodesian pilot, Douggie Leggo, bailed out of his crippled Spitfire and the Messerschmitt pilot who had shot him down, instead of flying away in the old "sportsman-like" fashion, swung back and collapsed Leggo's parachute with a burst of tracer bullets. Leggo plummeted to his death in the sea. Reprisal, as one would expect, was swift. Less than a week later a Canadian squadron-mate of Beurling's shot down a JU-88. After the three crewmen had climbed into a dinghy, the Canadian swept low over the water and riddled the helpless Germans with machine-gun fire. Lucas, who saw the incident, was appalled; he considered this kind of action nothing less than cold-blooded murder.

It's hard to say whether Beurling did that sort of thing himself. Lucas felt that it wasn't Beurling's style. However, a year later, Beurling had the following exchange with Canadian newspaperman Bruce West:

"George, did you ever shoot a guy in a parachute?"

"Yup," Beurling replied.

"A helpless guy in a parachute?" West asked incredulously.

"The way I figure it," Beurling continued, "he might get down, get back to Germany, and come back to shoot me down."

That may be. Still, Beurling's pronouncements to the press are not always to be believed. Nevertheless, the barbarous practice on both sides of murdering defenceless men grew throughout the war. Of course, it wasn't "official combatants" alone who were barbaric, as the pilot Stan Turner discovered.

One night Turner found himself sitting alone in a tiny bistro in the heart of Mdina when he spied three large clay pots behind the bar. The pots hadn't been there on his last visit and to make idle conversation with the bartender, Turner asked what was inside them. The bartender did not reply. Instead he lifted one of the lids and pulled up the severed head of a man. The head, the bartender explained with no remorse, belonged to a German pilot who, having bailed out safely over Malta, was attacked on the ground and butchered by a group of Maltese.

Everyone felt the black mood that summer and it is no wonder that Beurling himself, by October 1942, began to show signs of strain. Usually a reticent person on the ground, he suddenly began to talk constantly (one of the first symptoms of battle fatigue) and became even more obsessive over small details. Unfortunately, few of the other pilots were aware that Beurling was nearing his limits since they themselves were trying to cope under stress. The last thing a spooked pilot could recognize was the symptoms of combat fatigue in another.

So, October 14 dawned as another apparently routine day for George Beurling. Up before the sun, then aboard the battered bus, he journeyed down the hill for another day of combat flying. It was a tense morning of waiting, waiting for the dull rattle of the phone that would send the pilots running to their planes. The order came at 1300 hours, and down the Takali strip he roared once more into the flaming skies of Malta. Today's show was to the east, where fifty fighters and eight bombers were headed towards the island. For once, two entire squadrons of Spitfires were operational; the numbers gave them a little less than two-to-one odds. Not bad.

In the mêlée Beurling bagged three more German planes, one Junkers 88 and two Me-109's. But the young Canadian, who by now was regarded as some kind of wizard, made the near-fatal mistake of forgetting his own tail as he dove in to attack a Messerschmitt. Suddenly his Spitfire was rocked with cannon hits, and shrapnel struck his chest and his left heel and leg. With the controls shattered and the aircraft pitching into a 16,000-foot plunge, Beurling was certain he was going to die; but at 2,000 feet, with flames engulfing the cockpit, he managed to crawl out onto the wing, and at 500 feet he pulled the ripcord and floated to the sea, escaping from his fourth crash.

When the rescue launch reached him, Beurling was sitting in his rubber dinghy in a pool of blood. Back on the island, surgeons removed as much shrapnel as they could and patched up his left heel but the young Canadian had lost a portion of it, a wound which would plague him for the rest of his life. *

For the next two weeks Beurling lay in hospital near Takali, his foot and ankle in a cast, while surgeons picked away at the painful shrapnel wound. All the while he could see outside his hospital window the battle in the sky raging unabated. The Luftwaffe was now mounting its biggest attacks, a last brutal attempt to knock out Malta once and for all.

At the height of the bombing, on October 25, Beurling was surprised by a visit from the island's air officer commanding, Air Vice-Marshal Keith Park, who perhaps

* Buying shoes after the war became expensive. The only way Beurling could be comfortably fitted with new shoes was to buy two pair. The wound reduced his left foot to a size 10 while his right foot remained size 11 1/2.

more than anyone else was responsible for the tactics that enabled the RAF to win the Battle of Britain. As Beurling lay half-drugged in bed, the tough New Zealander told his most famous fighter that he had been awarded the Distinguished Service Order. Only days before the Canadian had been awarded the Distinguished Flying Cross, and since he already held the Distinguished Flying Medal and Bar, the award made an impressive array of "gongs", as RAF slang would term it. But these gongs raised no eyebrows; Beurling's kills since his arrival on Malta now stood at twenty-seven. This, added to a single kill and a probable in Europe, brought his total to twenty-nine. Park brought more than a decoration with him; he had bad news for Beurling. He was being sent home. The young ace angrily protested but Park overruled him. The request, he said, had come from the highest level of the Canadian government. Beurling was needed in Canada to take part in a recruiting campaign and the war bond drive.

Wounded and exhausted Beurling's remarkable Odyssey on the island was over. In Maltese he was "spicca" — finished.

Two days later, a few of his wingmates from 249 Squadron appeared at the hospital and carried him off to their hilltop lair for a farewell party. As night fell, they propped him in a chair on the terrace, a ringside seat for the nightly bombing. The attack was exceptionally heavy that evening and the formation of enemy fighters and bombers screaming over Malta created a live diorama of shell and fire. As the bombing reached its climax, Philip Lewis, an officer sitting near the ace, noticed that Beurling had become "extremely agitated". When Lewis remarked that all of this would be behind him, Beurling blurted out passionately, "I would do anything to fly."

"Even for the German?" Lewis asked light-heartedly.

"Yes," Beurling replied, "rather than be a prisoner."

It was a startling remark since pilots who had survived Malta combat usually left the island in a state of euphoria. Lewis became even more curious.

"Well, what are you going to do after the war, Screwball?"

"China," Beurling said without hesitation "I'll go to China. There's always a war there."

Beurling spent the night in Mdina in his old room in the palace on the hill. It was the end of his glory days. Gone was the excitement that was part of the dusty white heat of Malta, of the mottled Spitfires returning from combat, swinging over the Dingli cliffs, their ailerons dancing in the humid air. Gone was the whispering sea below their wings, a sea turned lava red by the evening sun.

At twenty-one years, gone, too, was George Beurling's youth. Cruelly, for the Knight of Malta, the worst was yet to come.

SEVEN

Coming Home

OVERNIGHT, George Beurling's name became as familiar to Canadians as Prime Minister Mackenzie King's, and his face as recognizable as any movie star's of the day. For a public weary of three grinding years of global conflict, Beurling was an attractive candidate for hero worship. He was the son every mother wanted, a decent kid who complained that he missed his mother's chocolate cake, a boy in an officer's uniform, and a publicist's dream. Not surprisingly, in anticipation of his homecoming, the press had begun to report his every move.

Following the night of the farewell party on the terrace, Beurling was shunted back and forth between the hospital and the airfield at Luqa waiting for a break in the bombing to begin his journey home. It came on November 1, 1942, when he was carried aboard a Liberator bomber for the first leg to Gibraltar. In addition to the normal six-man crew, there were eighteen passengers aboard, including two women, two babies, and another fighter pilot, A. H. Donaldson, who had been critically wounded in a dogfight the day after Beurling had been rescued from the sea.

The Liberator took off well before dawn, hugging the African shoreline as far as Algiers before it banked north to Gibraltar. When the bomber approached the Rock, the pilot discovered that site being battered by a raging thunderstorm. Short of fuel, and with no other place to land, the pilot was forced to try his luck; poor visibility caused him to miss two-thirds of the landing strip. Faced with the likelihood that he would overshoot the runway and crash into the sea, he opened up all four engines and prayed. The Liberator heaved into the air, managed to claw its way to an altitude of forty feet, then plunged like a stone into the water, killing everyone on board but the two fighter pilots, Donaldson and Beurling, and one other passenger. Beurling, who seemed to be making a habit of dramatic escapes, had done it again.*

As they approached the field Beurling had looked out to see what was happening. Sensing that the plane was in trouble he yanked the emergency-exit door open. "I felt her stalling," he told some student pilots a few months after the accident. "And as she actually stalled and started diving towards the sea, I jumped out. I hit just about the same time as the Liberator hit, but not in the aircraft."

Donaldson's version of the escape is different (he says they scrambled out after the Liberator hit the water); nevertheless, both miraculously survived. Beurling swam ashore where he collapsed and was rushed to the Gibraltar Military Hospital to be treated for shock. To make matters worse, the fractured heel was now showing signs of infection.

Meanwhile, the press back home in Canada and in England can be forgiven for making the most of Beurling's latest escape. The papers began to call him "Lucky" Beurling and, three days later, when he had been transferred to a hospital in England, reporters were around him as thick as mosquitoes. Every one of Beurling's few words ended up in print. He sat up in bed with a slice of bread and a cup of tea and urged the reporters "to make sure his mother knew that his leg wasn't broken". On November

* This was crash no. 5 and by far his luckiest escape from certain death.

7, George wrote his own byline for Canadian Press where he wondered "if my mother is pleased with what I've done".

Two days later he was put aboard another Liberator bomber in Prestwick, Scotland, and twenty-one hours later, after a stopover at the great Ferry Command base at Gander, Newfoundland, the young hero arrived at Montreal's Dorval Airport. There, in the cold darkness, he was re-united with his parents, his brothers, Richard and David, and his sister Gladys.

Still, the long flight was not over; in Ottawa, 120 miles away, Prime Minister King was preparing to greet the hero in the nation's capital. Beurling and his family were bundled aboard yet another aircraft that would take them on the short flight to Ottawa's Rockcliffe Airport.

At the Parliament Buildings in downtown Ottawa, the assembled press waited. At 6:15 p.m. a car filled with photographers screeched to a stop outside the portals of the East Block, followed minutes later by the car carrying Beurling. With his injured foot encased in a felt-like sock, he limped slowly out of the car and was blinded by a blaze of photographers' flash bulbs. It was a touching sight, according to *The Montreal Star*. "Reporters ordinarily calloused to headline figures," the *Star* reporter wrote, "rushed to help him. It was obvious he was a pretty tired hero." Who wouldn't be after a twenty-four-hour journey across the Atlantic?

No one could look on this slight figure, another writer said, without feeling that "here was a youth with hidden courage".

Although Mackenzie King astutely milked the moment for all it was worth, he almost made a terrible gaffe when he timed his arrival too late; Beurling was starting to weave in a faint while he stood waiting for the great man. Reporters quickly rushed a chair to him just as King arrived.

"I am delighted to see you," King said, shaking hands. "Warmest congratulations to you, not only on my behalf but on behalf of the people of Canada." Then King, noticing a group of beckoning photographers, added discreetly, "Now we have got to go outside and do all this over again."

Beurling hobbled to the camera positions and while the newsreel cameras whirred away, he stood patiently by while the moon-faced King held forth.

"May I say to you, Pilot-Officer Beurling, that had your arrival not been kept secret, these grounds would not have been big enough to hold the crowd wanting to see you. I did not come here to make a speech," King said, proceeding to do just that. During King's speech Beurling smiled his enigmatic smile.

"I have read in the press the fine things you have said about your mother and father," King said at one point, "and they have said equally fine things about you. It all reflects the fine training you have had in your home." The newsreel cameraman didn't like that take (too long) so they egged King on until they got the exchange they wanted.

Mr. King: "Tell me, Pilot-Officer Beurling, what is the secret of your great success?"

Beurling: "The upbringing my parents gave me."

The press, the secretaries from the Parliamentary offices, everyone in ear-shot was delighted as King turned to Beurling's mother and said, "That is a son to be proud of indeed." His mother replied quietly, "I am proud of him."

King departed, satisfied that he had exploited the moment for all its worth, his cherubic hands waving farewell, while Beurling was escorted to a nearby room for a news conference.

There he was modest and patient, answering the reporters' predictable questions with short, unemotional answers, none of which revealed to any extent the depth of the horror of Malta. Then the news conference broke up and Beurling, his tired eyes sunken, his face gaunt, struggled to a waiting taxi with his family.

"Their eager faces were etched in the darkness by a photographer's flash," a *Montreal Star* reporter wrote. "Then Beurling slumped into the far corner of the taxi. His mother stepped in quietly, letting him lean on her shoulder. The father got in and looked on silently. Their oldest boy was back in his mother's arms."

The next day Montreal and Verdun staged a welcome for the Knight of Malta worthy of royalty. It began at 11 a.m. with a news conference in the stately Windsor Hotel in Montreal. Later, as the day unfolded, a cold rain slashed the streets, but even so, eager crowds began to gather along the parade route from downtown Montreal to Verdun, where Beurling would be honoured that evening in the Verdun Auditorium.

By 7:45 p.m. thousands had jammed the streets around the hotel and when he walked from the front doors, a crowd surged towards him, cheering and clapping. The RCAF Ottawa Central Band, bussed in for the celebrations, struck up "For He's a Jolly Good Fellow" as the thin hero moved to a waiting limousine. The rain suddenly stopped, and the parade began to move north on Windsor Street, west on Ste Catherine, and down Atwater. Thousands shivered in the damp November night to catch a glimpse of the young pilot who, only a few months before, had been just another unknown serviceman. All along the parade route, the crowd surged from the curb and closed in on the passing car. Some boys even jumped on the running board, peering through the rain-misted windows for a glimpse of the hero. By the time he arrived in Verdun, 10,000 people had squeezed into the local ice rink. There was an explosion of applause and cheering when Beurling, lifted on the shoulders of two officers, was carried into the auditorium. He was borne to the end of the spacious hall and deposited on a painted plywood throne which had been erected on a dais. Two towering propellers had been placed on the wall above. Below the props was the figure "29", the total number of Beurling's kills (twenty-seven in Malta, two in Europe). Dozens of flags served as a backdrop. Below, on the floor of the arena, were massed the band and precision-drill platoons from the RCAF station at nearby Lachine along with a unit of the Women's Division, also bussed in from Ottawa.

A CBC announcer was there to broadcast the proceedings across Canada. The ceremony opened with the raising of the RCAF ensign, and a command that sent shivers through the crowd: "Trumpeters Sound the Still!"

Next, the popular mayor of Verdun, Edward Wilson, delivered a welcoming address, closing with words that would later sound especially poignant and haunting. "When peace is secured," Wilson said, turning to Beurling, "we trust that your days will be long in the land."

The RCAF, to their credit, did not dodge the issue of their rejection of Beurling early in the war. Air Commodore A. deNiverville, AOC No. 3 Training Command, told the throng, "There is no question about blind eyes when a certain lad from Verdun urged the RCAF to put him in uniform." The admission was punctuated with wild cheering and applause. The crowd had chosen sides. "This is one of the mistakes that the RCAF has made, and let us hope we will not make many more like that." Once more the crowd broke into delirious cheering. "We owe," deNiverville continued, "the Royal Air Force a debt for being wiser than we were and readily accepting him."

At last, it was Beurling's time to speak and silence fell on the crowd. In the hushed arena, he began, "This is no place for me. I'm a fighter pilot and not a speech-maker." The crowd loved it.

Growing up in Verdun, Quebec.

Beurling sold model airplanes to help pay for his flying
lessons.

ABOVE: Beurling (*third from the left*) with his wingmates at Takali airfield in Malta, the summer of 1942.

The Verdun boy in Malta. Probably the most published
photo of the ace.

LEFT: In Malta. As the summer passed Beurling's score
mounted.

In an English hospital, following combat in Malta. Beurling is showing the strains of battle, having lost fifty pounds in five months.

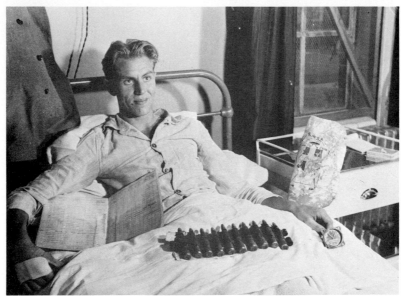

Beurling is greeted by his parents and younger brothers on his return from Malta. His sister Gladys and her husband, F.S. Hall, are on the right.

Moments before this photo was taken, Beurling nearly fainted from fatigue. He had been flown directly from hospital in England to Ottawa to meet Prime Minister King.

At the height of his fame, Beurling is carried into Verdun Auditorium, November 10, 1942.

Beurling, the uncomfortable hero, sits on the throne-like dais at his reception in the Verdun Auditorium.

A chocolate cake for his twenty-second birthday. His brothers, David (*left*) and Richard, help to cut the cake.

Frederick Beurling with his famous son.

Photo–Canada Wide

A charming smile hides the psychological scars of Malta combat.

"First of all," he continued, "you'll get a kick out of hearing that Canadian pilots in Malta are all doing a swell job. They are really great fellows and great fighters."

Beurling spoke for just over four minutes, his speech interrupted nine times by wild clapping and cheering. As he spoke his voice sounded curiously melancholy and fatigued. While he did not appear to have been infected with the crowd's exhilaration, Beurling didn't forget the other reasons for his being there.

"The other thing I wish to say is that while I haven't seen many newspapers, I did know there was a Victory Loan Drive and it was great news to hear that it had gone over the top. That will be a real thrill to the Canadians overseas, make them feel that everybody at home is backing them up."

Then he concluded: "I'm afraid, being kind of tired, that I didn't always look as though I was as thrilled as I actually have been. Things have been happening pretty fast these last few days, and I guess I'm a bit bewildered. At any rate, thanks so much for a wonderful welcome."

Next came the climax of the evening. To the accompaniment of ballet music, twenty-eight Girl Guides and a Brownie each presented the hero with a blood red rose — one for each of his kills.

It was intended, of course, that the girls with their roses would honour Beurling. Actually, this display was in dubious taste. Sadly, the blood-coloured flowers could not help but bring to the pilot's consciousness a nightmare that had been haunting him since leaving Malta.

On July 12, around noon, Beurling had within seconds bagged two Italian Macchi 202's. In one of the engagements, Beurling flew within thirty yards of the enemy aircraft. He could see that both the cockpit hood and the pilot's rear-view mirror had been shot away in an earlier skirmish. In a remarkable sound recording, which is in the Public Archives of Canada, Beurling has recounted the incident in detail:

> I came right up underneath his tail. I was going faster than
> he was; about fifty yards behind. I was tending to over-
> shoot. I weaved off to the right, and he looked out to his
> left. I weaved to the left and he looked out to his right. So,
> he still didn't know I was there. About this time I closed up
> to about thirty yards, and I was on his portside coming in at
> about a fifteen-degree angle. Well, twenty-five to thirty
> yards in the air looks as if you're right on top of him
> because there is no background, no perspective there and it
> looks pretty close. I could see all the details in his face
> because he turned and looked at me just as I had a bead on
> him.

For an instant the frantic eyes of the doomed pilot met
the piercing eyes of the man who was about to take his life.
Beurling fired a single burst that decapitated the pilot. The
body, still strapped in the cockpit of the Macchi, continued to pump blood through the severed jugular. The
blood was caught in the slipstream and was flattened like
slow-moving syrup against the camel-coloured fuselage.
The effect is one known to any jet traveller today watching raindrops turned to liquid film on an airliner's window. The blood flowed over the fuselage until it obliter-
ated the white cross on the aircraft's tail.

"One of my can shells caught him right in the face and
blew his head right off," Beurling recounts in the recording. "The body slumped and the slipstream caught the
neck, the stub of the neck, and the blood streamed down
the side of the cockpit."

Throughout this description Beurling's voice appears
remorseless and unfeeling. "It was a great sight anyway,"
he concludes, "the red blood down the white fuselage. I
must say it gives you a feeling of satisfaction when you

actually blow their brains out."

His public bravado, however, masked private sorrow. According to Beurling's youngest brother, David, the painful memory of this incident left George with nightmares that made him "cry all night". This is a surprising revelation, not only in light of Beurling's own words, but also in light of the hard-hearted, ruthless killer that others came to perceive him to be. Probably he liked to think he was genuinely remorseless where really he was not. He certainly did all in his power to prevent word of his torments and tears from leaving the family. The family admits to this day no more that the simple but moving fact that George suffered nightmares after his return; beyond that they'll give away nothing.

We are left, then, with Beurling's and the press's mythmaking. Here, for instance, is a portion of the statement he gave a group of newsmen in Ottawa during his first interview in Canada:

> I wonder if he [the enemy] is going to blow or fry. There is no time for any other kind of thought. There is always someone on your tail and you have to be pretty sharp. There is not time to loiter around. You have to be hard-hearted, too. You must blaze away whenever you are in a position to get his oxygen bottles or gas tanks.

In addition to the emotional scars, the Verdun hero was also a physical wreck. He was seriously undernourished; the meagre diet on Malta had literally left him starved. His wounds had festered, and within a few days of the reception, Beurling had to be secretly admitted to the Royal Victoria Hospital in Montreal, where the doctors, taking pity on him, allowed him a brief visit home to celebrate his twenty-second birthday. His mother, who had been saving her sugar ration, baked his favourite chocolate cake.

For weeks air-force signals poured from Ottawa to Montreal urgently asking when Beurling would be fit enough to begin the war bond tour. Prime Minister King got his wish in mid-February when Beurling, his health greatly improved, left for a hectic, month-long tour of Canada, a coast-to-coast trip totalling 6,000 miles. He appeared at service flight-training schools, army camps, and numerous factories. He made pleas for Canadians to buy Victory Bonds and encouraged enlistment.

Before long, he came to resent his promotional duties. He was convinced that both the RCAF and the Liberal government were exploiting him.

"If I were ever asked to do that again," he said afterward, rather cynically, "I'd tell them to go to hell, or else ask for a commission on the bonds I sold."

Yet, while the show was on the road, he bore the ordeal silently, perhaps because he had discovered that the tour had its compensations. Since his arrival home in November 1942, the flattery of the press and the public adulation were not without effect. We can, in fact, safely say that his reputation as a lady's man began on the bond tour.

Women found him enormously handsome in his tailored RAF uniform with his load of decorations, and they pursued him at every stop across the country. Reporters covering Beurling were naturally quick to notice that the hero did not spurn the affection. For instance, Charles Lynch (who later became a war correspondent and after the war a press celebrity) recalls stumbling into a room in Halifax and finding Beurling locked in a passionate embrace with a local beauty atop a Ping-Pong table.

Near the end of the tour, in Vancouver in March 1943, the tables were turned on Beurling. He was holding a news conference at Jericho Beach in a room that was obviously too small to hold everyone who had gathered there for a look at the hero. Beurling, for his part, couldn't keep his eyes off an attractive brunette, a messenger at Western Command. He quickly found out her name. She was Diana Eve Whittall, a west-coast debutante, the daughter of a respected Vancouver family, and the widow of an RAF flight lieutenant named Edwin Gardner (he had been killed in 1939 when his plane crashed returning from a bombing mission). Beurling telephoned the young widow that same evening and, against the protest of her parents, she accepted his invitation for dinner.

"We talked a lot about his war exploits," Diana recalled many years later. "He was really wound up. He had all this nervous energy, all this compressed energy inside him. He talked mostly about himself but I found it really fascinating."

The following night they went to a movie and after they left the theatre on Georgia Street opposite the Hudson's Bay store, Beurling began to serenade her.

"He sang 'Moonlight Becomes You'. He had a lovely voice and he actually sounded like Bing Crosby. He was very romantic," Diana recalls. "He used to like to scare women, frighten them with some of the most ghastly stories. He told one about the head rolling past him [the decapitation of the Italian pilot]. It was just awful. The girls would listen so intently and then when he got to the punchline they would all scream and gasp, and he would just roar with laughter."

A day or two later, they had become fast friends, and Diana soon discovered how much of a celebrity Beurling had become when they kept a swimming date at Vancouver's Crystal Pool.

"He had everyone gasping at him," Diana remembers. "He was doing all these fancy dives. People were just fascinated, and when they realized who it was, they watched and watched. He put on quite a display of swimming and diving. He knew that he could create that kind of sensation. He was absolutely charming."

Near the end of March 1943 Beurling left Vancouver to continue his bond-selling tour. Although he never wrote to Diana after leaving the west coast, some fourteen months later he would telephone her to propose marriage and Diana would accept.

By the spring of 1943, the hero of Malta was eager to return to combat; he was quite a different person from the shy loner who had left Canada three years before.

The handsome fighter pilot had become Canada's best-known serviceman. In spite of his success, Beurling nevertheless complained bitterly of the demands the tour made on him, and began to openly condemn the RCAF for exploiting his heroism to sell war bonds.

He had an additional gripe against the RCAF. The Canadians, his story goes, had pressed the British to have him transferred out of his beloved RAF and into the RCAF because they wanted him for themselves. Examination of official RCAF records, however, indicates that Beurling himself asked to be transferred. Shortly after the promotion tour ended, Beurling wrote a letter to Air Commodore deNiverville (who had publicly apologized for the RCAF at the Verdun reception) telling him, "It has been long my wish that I transfer from the RAF to the RCAF." The letter, in a most conciliatory tone, continues:

Unfortunately it appears that a wrong impression has got around that because of the fact the RCAF refused my enlistment, I have no use for it. That is entirely wrong. Since returning to Canada I have wanted such a transfer. Some time ago Air Minister Power stated in public that the RCAF had made a big blunder in having refused my enlistment. I had thought of going to Ottawa to see Mr. Power and tell him that he could easily rectify this mistake by securing my transfer to the RCAF. . . . As you are aware sir, I have, in whatever way I could, given assistance to the RCAF personnel since my return and have willingly accepted the responsibility of touring stations to advise instructors and students in flying tactics. If this has been of value to them, I am satisfied. I would appreciate the opportunity of working with my own country's air force.

DeNiverville acted immediately by writing to RCAF headquarters in Ottawa and recommending that they respond to Beurling's request; he pointed out that the officer's services during the tour of Canada "were invaluable". Because Beurling, now confirmed in the rank of flying officer, was still a member of the RAF, protocol required the Royal Air Force's acquiescence which, given wartime bureaucracy, did not come until July. The RAF then decided that September 1, 1943, would be the day Beurling was to be sworn in to the RCAF.

EIGHT

The Living Legend

THE RETURN TO BATTLE began in New York City. The hero sailed for England aboard the *Queen Elizabeth* which left its Hudson River pier on May 5, 1943.

On board ship was Bruce West, the Toronto news-paperman who had been seconded from *The Globe and Mail* for a so-called "homburg" assignment in London with the Wartime Information Board. His curiosity as a reporter drew him to Beurling as the ship set sail. West liked the young man the moment they met; he found Beurling easy-going and especially enjoyed his sense of humour.

Several days into the crossing Beurling appeared in West's crowded cabin with an enormous grin on his face. "Aren't you going to congratulate me?" he asked.

The question left West puzzled until Beurling announced that he had "just got married" to an American nurse he had met on board; a special ceremony had been performed by the ship's captain.

The rumour quickly spread throughout the troopship; it was not until a few hours later that West and the other passengers learned that they had had their legs pulled. An announcement on the ship's public-address system denied that any such nuptials had taken place.

The coverage by the British press began as soon as the *Queen Elizabeth* docked in Glasgow and Beurling disembarked for London. A unique ceremony in his honour was being arranged at Buckingham Palace. King George VI waited to bestow on Beurling the awards so hard won in Malta—the DSO, DFC, and DFM and Bar. At the time he was the first fighting man to be given four decorations at once at a Royal Investiture. On the day of the ceremony, Beurling was whisked to the palace gates where he ambled inside under the Grand Entrance portico and into the Grand Hall; the King was waiting to greet him.

"How was Malta?" His Majesty inquired, when the young ace approached.

"I enjoyed every minute of it, sir," Beurling replied candidly.

Meanwhile, word of his appearance at the palace had drawn a crowd and by the time Beurling emerged from the ceremony there was a hopeless traffic jam. Somehow, the Canadian had managed to discover two good-looking American servicewomen inside the palace. He set off into the mob with a pretty girl on each arm. One of the women, Jean Johnson, a nurse from Ohio, was soon separated from her famous escort by the photographers, autograph-hunters, and other women admirers who surrounded the much-decorated hero.

He was big news, a story sweetened by the disclosure from Beurling that he'd been unable to find a hotel room the night before and therefore had been forced to spend the night on a park bench in front of the palace.

Meanwhile, Beurling waited to see what the Royal Air Force intended to do with him before his transfer to the RCAF. Wisely, it was decided not to post him to an operational squadron; there was concern that the great ace would be shot down. Instead, the RAF posted Beurling to its Central Gunnery School at Sutton Bridge where, as an instructor, his talents as the world's master of the deflection shot would be put to good use.

The posting, with its teaching load and make-believe dogfights, bored Beurling until one day one of the training sessions turned out to have serious consequences. Beurling was shot down—not by the enemy but by a fellow pilot.

Beurling was engaged in a mock dogfight when the student pilot accidently fired his loaded guns and hit Beurling's engine. Soon the engine coolant of his Spitfire exploded in flames, forcing the teacher to bail out at 1,400 feet.* Because he pulled the ripcord too soon, Beurling's parachute was damaged; luckily it opened when he was 600 feet from the ground.

Later Beurling confided to Bruce West that the student pilot was in fact not a student but another Canadian ace, Flight Lieutenant Robert Buckham. There is no way to check the story since Buckham was later killed in a flying accident.

After Beurling had parachuted safely to the ground, he returned to the gunnery school and reported that his tank had sprung a leak and he had been forced to bail out. He and the "student" never discussed the incident.

This escape was only the first of three that occurred at Sutton Bridge in as many months. The second happened during what is called a "fighter take-off", a manoeuvre in which the pilot is required to retract the undercarriage as quickly as possible. In this particular instance, Beurling tried to bring the wheels up before they had cleared the runway; the undercarriage collapsed and the Spitfire belly-flopped onto the ground. The plane was heavily damaged.

The third crash involved a forced landing in the tidal flatland of the Wash. Wilfrid Aldrich, a RAF pilot who was flying an aged Wellington over the sand banks, was

* Escape no. 6.

amused to see Beurling stamping out a message in the sand next to his crippled Spitfire as the incoming tide crept around him. "You may land here," he signalled. Unfortunately there were no takers, and his rescue was left to local boatmen. (Total crashes to date: eight.)

Beurling saw Bruce West frequently that summer of 1943, spending weekends in the flat above the Phoenix Theatre on Charing Cross Road that West shared with Canadian war correspondent Andy O'Brien.

"He was a lonely lad," West recalls. "His biography was running in the London *Daily Express*, but despite all the publicity he was just as lonely and lost as any soldier." During those weekend leaves, Beurling slept on a safari cot in the flat and shared the occupants' meagre rations, once demolishing a pound of over-ripened Oka cheese.

Beurling frequently accompanied West to his favourite local, the Coach and Horses on Greek Street in Soho, where Beurling drank ginger ale. Another hangout and drinking spot was the Haymarket Club. On one occasion, West reports, "there was a Canadian major sitting in the corner with some others and he came over to our table. 'So you're Flying Officer Beurling,' he said with a slight English accent. And Beurling said, 'Yes, sir.' 'Well,' the major said, 'my group and I have decided to let you join us over there.' He was half kidding, yet pompous at the same time. Beurling just looked at the man, then turned his back to him, completely ignoring him. Beurling wasn't exactly a pukka-sahib officer. In fact he looked as if he slept in his clothes."

But West's most vivid memory was of Beurling's restlessness with his instructor's job and his impatience to get back into combat. As the day drew closer when he would be formally transferred to the RCAF, Beurling's eagerness grew. "I've never been better," he told West. "I can hit a teacup at 300 yards."

Finally the day of his swearing-in arrived and, at 9 a.m. on September 1, 1943, Beurling shuffled into the imposing headquarters of the RCAF in London, a stone's throw from the august Lincoln's Inn Fields law courts.

The assembled brass took an anxious look and heaved a collective sigh. Beurling was wearing a battered hat with the rim stiffener removed.

"Get him a hat," ordered Air Vice-Marshal W. A. Curtis. The official RCAF photographer, Vic Davidson, obligingly handed over his more presentable headgear, then stepped back, raised his Newman Sinclair 35mm newsreel camera and pressed the shutter trigger. The prodigal son had come home.

The new alliance between the casual, not to say sloppy, Beurling and the more formal RCAF was a sensitive one. There's no doubt that the Canadian government was making political gain out of Beurling's transfer to the RCAF. He had become the darling of King's Liberal party in Canada and King's personal hero. But now the RCAF brass was stuck with him. Mindful of his record at 41 Squadron before his Malta days and aware, too, of Beurling's penchant for flaunting his individuality, the RCAF was in a delicate position. A portent of what lay ahead came that very first day when Beurling casually mentioned to reporters that he had spent yet another night on a park bench under a horse chestnut tree in front of RCAF headquarters. The RCAF was not well-organized, he suggested coyly, if it couldn't provide lodgings for its most visible officer. The RCAF was also to learn quickly what it probably already suspected: the hot shot from Verdun was insufferably arrogant. More worrisome to the brass, however, was the potential for conflict between Beurling and his wingmates, who rightly feared that the ace would try to hog all the headlines.

To ensure against this, a memorandum was issued

barely eight days after Beurling joined the RCAF. Air Marshal H. "Gus" Edwards told his staff of press-relations officers that "further publicity concerning this officer is to be withheld". Although Beurling's skill as a fighter was highly regarded, there remained official doubt about his unorthodox approach to discipline.

The RCAF, after much thought, decided to post him to 403 Squadron, the squadron in which he had served after leaving OTU in December 1941. The squadron was now part of the RCAF's 127 Wing and, in September 1943, it was commanded by one of Britain's most famous fighter pilots, Johnnie Johnson. Johnson, a Briton much in the same mold as Beurling's first flight commander in Malta, Laddie Lucas, was tough and decisive, enough so to handle, so authorities thought, their Canadian mustang. The brass arranged an informal meeting between Beurling and Johnson a few days before Beurling's formal transfer to the RCAF. On a warm August day, Beurling drove down to an airfield in Kent and presented himself to Johnson. They chatted casually but Johnson's message was clear; it was essentially the same as Lucas's many months earlier. "There is one rule," Johnson said firmly, "and it is not to be broken. We always fight as a team." There would be no lone-wolf stuff in 403. Beurling apparently agreed and the meeting ended. Johnson was pleased with what seemed to be an amiable beginning.

In September 1943, the tide of battle had turned in the Allies' favour on the world's battlefronts. That summer the invasion of Sicily had been successfully launched, and two days before Beurling went back on operations, the Italian mainland had been broached. That August the Quebec Conference had approved the timetable for "Operation Overlord", the invasion of France. But most important for Beurling, the U.S. Eighth Air Force had begun its strategic bombardment of German industry, an undertaking that relied heavily on fighter support. The Canadian 127 Wing, to which 403 Squadron belonged, had become a vital part of the operation, mounting all of its thirty-six aircraft to provide an umbrella of protection for the daylight raids. Casualties were high. Many of the pilots were young, inexperienced, and poor shots. In addition, many of them simply ran out of gas over France while returning from escort missions. *

One day in early September, Beurling appeared, ready for duty with 403, a celebrated figure who made an immediate mark on the squadron.

One of the other pilots, Robert Hyndman (who later became an official Canadian war artist, and in civilian life a noted portrait painter) was drawn immediately to the new arrival.

Beurling struck Hyndman as a dreamer who, in spite of his reputation as an insensitive hired gun, seemed disarmingly gentle. As an artist he immediately noticed Beurling's unusual eyes. Naturally he wanted to sketch Beurling but whenever the artist approached him Beurling's gaze made Hyndman feel he was intruding. The artist said there was something of the "poet" about Beurling, the upturned collar of his battle jacket, the longer-than-regulation haircut, but most of all Beurling's reluctance about being examined, especially by someone as perceptive as an artist. Instead Hyndman viewed Beurling from afar, wondering to himself what was the special quality about the ace that defied definition. Like so many others, he never found an adequate answer. **

* Few factors in flying vary so much as the amount of fuel that an airplane consumes. It can vary dramatically, depending on wind direction, altitude, and airspeed. All pilots must constantly weigh these factors for their safety.

* * Hyndman never did sketch or paint Beurling. The missed opportunity is one of Hyndman's few regrets as an artist. One of the last

When Beurling joined the squadron, it was operating out of Headcorn in Kent. There was a transient gloom about the place. The pilots lived in tents, and the airstrip itself suggested impermanent occupancy with its hastily laid sections of wire-mesh runways.

Although not as rakish as 249 Squadron, 403 still bore all the earmarks of a warriors' camp. Fitters scrambled over the Spitfires like chicks around the mother hen. Supply trucks raced to and fro about the base, splashing mud on officers and ground crews with equal disregard for rank. The pilots looked like extras on a Hollywood movie lot, sporting automatic pistols in hip holsters. Battered hats, rumpled tunics, and muddy flight boots were familiar trappings. Most mornings the men climbed out of bed long before it was light for a breakfast of dehydrated eggs. They waited for what always seemed an eternity around the pot-bellied stove in the dispersal hut, frequently to be told that the operation was cancelled because of lousy weather.

Beurling felt at home for he had been warmly welcomed by the young squadron commander, Hugh Godefroy, twenty-four. Godefroy told Beurling that his greatest contribution to 403 would be to sharpen the marksmanship skills of the newly arriving and green replacement pilots. Soon Beurling had established shooting-angle practice, replacing the Takali lizards with a model of a Me-109 mounted on a swivel post. A pilot was placed in a wooden chair about twelve feet from the target. At approximately 300 yards, a real Me-109 would appear the same size from the cockpit of a Spitfire. One of these pilots

times Hyndman saw the hero was on V-E Day in the lobby of the Mount Royal Hotel in Montreal. Hyndman was left saddened when he sensed that Beurling was "entirely disenchanted" with civilian life.

was Andy MacKenzie, a rugged Montrealer, who vividly remembers his lessons.

"He'd adjust the model and ask me to call off the angles," MacKenzie recalls. "He'd say that the fleeing airplane is going such and such a speed and he'd move the model around to different positions, each time asking me to guess the angle. I made up a chart on a Sweet Caporal cigarette package and actually stuck it in the cockpit of my Spitfire. I studied it religiously."

The lessons had an extraordinary affect on MacKenzie's marksmanship. Within a few weeks he had shot down three enemy airplanes.

"In just weeks I had three of them burning in twenty seconds. Christ, I couldn't believe it. It was like shooting ducks. It was so easy. It happened so fast that I got a gong by telephone." MacKenzie says once he "got onto a pair of them. The guy on the tail, I remember, was looking back at me. I mean it was over for him. I saw him talking to his leader. Maybe those were his last words. He was gone. I went after the leader and in ten seconds he was finished too. Then I got the third just as easily."

All the while, Johnnie Johnson watched over Beurling's activities with satisfaction. Perhaps the lone wolf wasn't going to be that difficult after all, he thought.

As was the usual practice, the wing leader rotated from squadron to squadron. One day Johnson came to lead 403 on a sweep over France. The flight went normally for a while, but then suddenly and without warning, the Canadian broke from his section and headed for the ground, strafing anything that moved. Johnson exploded. Back at the airstrip he told Beurling that his independent action had not only been "stupid" but more important it had set a "bad example to the remainder of the junior pilots in the Wing".

Beurling apologized (he had learned how to do that) and

the tension eased — for the moment.

A few days later, Beurling "borrowed" Johnson's favourite shotgun and went stalking birds. His unerring marksmanship brought two down in quick succession, but unfortunately he had managed to kill the only extant pair of Great Crested Grebe in southern England. Again, Beurling found himself on the carpet for what Johnson felt was his "frightful behaviour".

Although Johnson left the Wing a short time later, Beurling's problems with authority were by no means over. The new superior officer was Hugh Godefroy, now a wing commander. In no time Godefroy discovered how much trouble he had inherited. One day, while 403 was on another routine sweep, the squadron was suddenly directed to intercept an incoming force of twenty raiders. An advance radar station on the coast of the Channel had positioned 403 above and behind the F-W 190's, a letter-perfect position to bounce the marauding Germans. As 403 gained on the enemy, the pilots could hardly believe that their approach was still undetected. Godefroy checked his flock one last time just before leading it onto the pack below. He was astonished to see Beurling flying upside down! Then just as unbelievably, Beurling's Spitfire plunged earthward, leaving the squadron hanging above. In the twists and rolls of combat that followed, Godefroy heard Beurling's voice croak over the radio, "I've had it." Minutes later, 403 was screaming back to the peaceful countryside of Kent, its members convinced that somehow Beurling had "bought it".

Fifteen minutes later, a lone Spitfire moved gently into the circuit and landed with feather softness. It was Beurling. Godefroy was, of course, steaming with anger as he hiked across the runway but his anger drained instantly when he came face to face with Beurling, who was weaving uneasily, seemingly in a trance. The whites of Beurling's eyes, now turned crimson red, presented such a bizarre image that Godefroy was left speechless. It became obvious what had happened.

Beurling had been flying a Spitfire Mark IXb, perhaps the most demanding of the Vickers models. He had broken formation to go after a lone German skimming far below over the water, a target that appealed to him more than the gaggle of 190's. Unfortunately, because he had misjudged the enormous power of the new Mark IXb, the dive he had put himself into quickly became so steep and fast that Beurling was unable to bring his aircraft back to level flight. The crushing force of gravity made him lose consciousness. The pressure was so severe that the blood vessels of his eyeballs hemorrhaged. As the water loomed closer, Beurling somehow regained consciousness, only to discover that the controls of the aircraft were frozen. Too weak to abandon the aircraft, Beurling took one last chance and delicately teased the trim tabs on the tail. Slowly, miraculously, the Spitfire regained level flight.

Godefroy and the other pilots discovered, when they inspected the Spitfire, that every rivet had been popped and the metal skin had wrinkled like a piece of corrugated cardboard.* The Spitfire was, of course, scrapped and Beurling was subjected to a mild reprimand. Godefroy felt that the young pilot's brush with death was punishment enough.

Soon it was October and the chill English autumn bored into the fliers' bones. In the middle of the month, it was time for the squadron to leave the soggy tents at Headcorn and fly to winter quarters at Kenley, in Surrey. While stationed at Headcorn, Beurling had managed to add only one more kill to his score, an F-W 190. He grew

---

* Several pilots told the author that it was amazing Beurling was able to land the Spitfire because it was so badly damaged. Escape no. 9.

increasingly sour and uncommunicative. All he wanted
was action in the air; all he found was misunderstandings
with his superiors.

The misunderstandings stemmed from Beurling's
refusal to stay in formation. The kind of fighting he had
experienced in Malta was entirely different from what he
found in England. The whole nature of the battle in the air
had changed. About the time he got to 403, the RCAF brass
had decided there would be no more "rhubarbs", the
patrols which took pilots into France, Belgium, and Holland looking for targets. These were always low-level
strafing affairs against enemy trains, truck convoys, and
troop concentrations. While "heart-in-the-mouth" exciting, the operations were exceedingly dangerous. Casualties began to mount on the so-called "rhubarbs", victims
of ground fire as well as German fighter interruption. The
low-level intrusions became too expensive in terms of lost
men and machines. They were abandoned.

More important, however, was the fact that the fighters
were needed as protection for the awesome daylight
bomber operations being stepped up by the Americans.
Beurling nevertheless found escorting these massed formations something akin to herding sheep. He was bored
and he made no attempt to disguise his feelings.

Matters did not improve at the squadron's new base. In
fact, Beurling's hostility came to be focused more and
more on his own comrades. Once, at the dispersal hut,
several pilots sat and watched while a lone Spitfire, piloted
by a green replacement, staggered onto the airstrip for an
embarrassingly bad landing. The plane bounced, once,
twice, and then a third time. All the while, Beurling
screamed over and over: "Crash!...Crash!...Crash!...
You deserve to die for that landing." Beurling's words
carried such conviction that a stunned silence came over
the usually noisy hut, a spell that was not broken until

THE LIVING LEGEND • 103

another pilot said to Beurling quietly, "He's on our side, George."

Impossible flying weather frequently kept the pilots on the ground in October, giving them more time on their hands than they knew what to do with. Not far from 403's mess, a lovely vine-covered house, lay a small pond, inhabited by a friendly wood duck which had been tamed by Robert Buckham, the pilot who had shot Beurling down at Sutton Bridge. Buckham was a quiet youngster from Vancouver. In a number of ways his personality resembled Beurling's; he too was withdrawn and reticent. He loved flowers, birds, and animals, and he loved especially his tame duck, which he fed with scraps from his own plate. One day, while Godefroy was sitting outside the mess enjoying a cigarette, Beurling ambled out, walked to the duck pond, and studied the bird. Slowly he unholstered his Smith and Wesson .38 and began to fire rapidly at the startled duck. At that instant Buckham emerged from the mess door white with rage. He dashed across the grass and with one lightning move kicked the revolver from Beurling's hand, sending it clattering into a nearby rock garden.

Before any of the startled pilots could react, Buckham grabbed Beurling by the throat and hissed, "If you ever do that again I'll kill you with my bare hands." Beurling backed off; everyone knew that Buckham was a judo expert.

"I was only shooting off his tail feather, Buck," Beurling said weakly. Godefroy attributed the flare-up to the enormous tension the fighter pilots lived with daily. He put the incident out of his mind and turned to more pressing matters. With so many young pilots arriving as replacements, there was a desperate shortage of experienced pilots of Beurling's calibre. Out of necessity he recommended Beurling for promotion to the rank of flight lieutenant. Naturally Beurling objected, saying he didn't want the paperwork that went with the job of running the flight. There was, on the other hand, one nice perk that went with the assignment. Because the squadron's Tiger Moth (which was used as a messenger aircraft between the squadrons in the Wing) would come under Beurling's charge, he decided to accept the promotion. Soon the Moth, a slow but delicately responsive training biplane, became Beurling's pride and joy.

Not one to be idle between fighter sorties, he flew the Moth every chance he could. For example, he made early-morning flights to neighbouring farms, missions that kept him supplied with fresh eggs while everyone else on the station was stuck with the powdered kind.

The Moth, however, became the instrument of his next confrontation with authority. Although a spell of rotten weather had grounded the Spitfires during the first week in November, it didn't prevent Beurling from taking the Moth up for some strictly forbidden aerobatics over the airfield. When Godefroy hear the tiny plane groaning over his office, he sent orders to the dispersal hut for Beurling to come to him when he landed. Their relations had soured ever since Beurling "wrote-off" one Spitfire in his mad dive in September.

"Look, Beurling," Godefroy said patiently, "I'm responsible for air discipline around here and if you want to do low flying, go somewhere I can't see you. But not over the airfield."

But two days later, Beurling was back in the air over the station; minutes after this second performance he was back in Godefroy's office.

"For Christ's sake," Godefroy told him one more time, "don't do it."

The next day Beurling was at it a third time. The ceiling was down to 300 feet that day, when suddenly the Moth appeared out of the murk headed for Godefroy's office window, so low that one of its wings cleared the dew off the grass.

Godefroy's patience was exhausted. When Beurling shuffled into the wing commander's office, Godefroy finally blew up. "What the hell are you doing?" he yelled.

Beurling leaned against the door, slowly raised his finger at his commanding officer, and in a whisper-quiet voice spoke.

"You," he said, "you can't tell me what to do."

Beurling's insubordination momentarily stunned Godefroy.

"That plane," Beurling continued, "is under my command, in my flight."

Godefroy didn't believe what he was hearing; Beurling had left him with only one choice.

"You're under open arrest," he told the ace. "Get out." Since it was the first step leading to a court martial, the charge carried the most serious implications.

When news reached RCAF headquarters in London there was swift, angry reaction; within hours, Air Marshal "Gus" Edwards, the man who had ordered the publicity blackout around Beurling, was yelling on the phone into Godefroy's ear. "What the hell are you doing down there?" he shouted.

After Godefroy had explained what had happened, he asked Edwards whether there was any other choice he could have made.

"No choice?" the Air Marshal retorted. "Don't you know the prime minister has just crowned him King of Canada!"

But Godefroy stood firm and defended his action.

What followed next is cloudy, but it appears that the Minister of Air, Charles Gavan "Chubby" Power, interceded on Beurling's behalf and reduced his sentence from open arrest to grounding.

RCAF headquarters in London reported back to Ottawa

that "Beurling was conscious of the minister's interest" and that he accepted "discipline willingly and cheerfully" —a rather gratuitous remark considering that the alternative was a full-blown court martial, which would not only embarrass Beurling but also the Liberal government that had taken him under its wing, and which needed no more problems than it already had.

In Canada, Mackenzie King was walking a tightrope. That September he had promised Quebec that the government would never enforce overseas conscription, yet there were many rumours that, with the mounting casualties in Italy, King would have to implement overseas conscription unless he could get enough volunteers to fill the depleted fighting ranks. The last thing King needed was the spectacle of a court martial of Canada's famous warrior over what the public would consider a misdemeanour. Instead, Beurling would be grounded. That way everyone could get off the hook.

So, on November 7, 1943, Beurling was hustled out of 403 into 412 Squadron; the next day the news broke that he was grounded.

Beurling had become a celebrity and he knew how to put this setback to good use. He got in touch with the journalist friends he had been courting in his boyish and charming way. The press, for its part, treated Beurling like the star he had become. They pandered to him in the same way that today's sports journalists pamper recalcitrant superathletes in their negotiations with team management over contract disputes. Besides, Beurling was exciting copy, unpredictable, colourful and, in contemporary jargon, sexy. They delighted in writing about him, especially about his frequent and very public romances. At this time they were reporting that he was about to marry. The girl was a brown-eyed Canadian student living in London, Kathleen Marie Clough-Ormiston. Though the reports state that the couple had applied for a marriage licence at the Marylebone Register's Office, a search of the records today shows no such entry.

Kathleen would not be the last woman Beurling pursued. Why Beurling engaged in this compulsive prowling is a matter of speculation. It is possible that he turned to it out of restlessness. He simply was not flying enough and what flying he did was not the kind he thought a fighter pilot should do.

The truth was fighter pilots were lucky if they got in 300 hours of flying time per year. The weather was frequently bad which meant the squadrons were grounded. The English day was short, dawn arriving late and dusk swift and early. The pilots needed daylight to operate.

At his new station Beurling became more and more restless, thinking up any number of antics to occupy his time and to serve as a release for his boundless energy.

When he arrived at 412 Squadron at Biggin Hill he took over as commander of A flight. As such he got control of one of the flight's heavy-duty trucks which was used to transport the pilots about the airfield. One of his wingmates, D. J. "Dewey" Dewan, remembers it was worth the pilots' lives to ride when Beurling was behind the wheel. Dewan recalls that once Beurling tried to deposit his passengers at the very doorstep of the dispersal hut by slamming on the brakes at the last possible moment as the truck hurtled towards the building. He then turned the steering wheel violently to one side, trying to put the vehicle into a four-wheel drift. The truck turned 180 degrees and slid backwards towards the door. He was the first out to check to see how close he had come, all the time laughing uproariously.

His absences were noticed. Thinking he had gone on a weekend leave his wingmates were surprised when he appeared one Monday morning sporting a very visible suntan. Beurling explained with quiet delight that he had spent the weekend in the Azores — courtesy of an American pilot he had met who had invited him aboard his Liberator for a couple of days in the sun.

Not all his wingmates were enamoured of the ace. One of them felt he could be thoughtless and vulgar. Bill McCrae was astonished the day that Beurling rose at the mess table and read aloud the contents of some girl's maudlin love letter.

"Its contents," McCrae said, "would have given me ulcers." After Beurling finished reading it, he casually tossed the letter into the mess fireplace.

As 1943 neared its end, Beurling's hope of seeing more combat was briefly realized in December when he shot down a F-W 190. This was to be his last victory in combat.*

The next four months found him again growing restive, for the pattern of battle in the air had not changed. The Canadian Wing continued operating en masse in close support of the lumbering American bombers as they droned day after day to the continent, blasting away at Hitler's European fortress. The Canadian, of course, longed for a revival of the freewheeling Malta-style combat; besides, the RCAF finally had him on a short leash and were closely screening press releases that mentioned the ace.

Of course, there was no way to keep Beurling quiet for long. In March 1944, he came up with a sensational plan that he believed would give him back the kind of combat he longed for. He wanted to form his own flight, not of Spitfires but of long-range American Mustang fighters. He saw himself as a kind of airborne privateer, striking deep into occupied France or perhaps even into Germany

* See Appendix.

itself, taking on all comers. All the while he would himself be protected by three hand-picked wingmates who would fly shotgun for the lone ranger of the RCAF.

He asked for and was granted a meeting at RCAF Headquarters in London with the newly appointed Air Officer Commander-in-Chief, Air Marshal L. S. Breadner. A corporal in the Women's Division assigned to headquarters remembers the day Beurling appeared at the meeting. "He acted like he was a god," Joyce Skene said years later.

Beurling's request to form his own flying circus was, not surprisingly, rejected out of hand. There were no witnesses at the meeting and details of what transpired are hearsay. Beurling later told Andy MacKenzie that he had called Breadner a "black-hearted sonofabitch". For the RCAF the Beurling problem remained. Some RCAF members were beginning to wonder what this madman might do next.

Breadner's rejection was the final blow for Beurling. Within weeks he formally asked to be repatriated to Canada. For the RCAF this must have seemed a mercifully quick and convenient solution to a situation that was becoming impossible.

But according to Britain's great fighter, Johnnie Johnson, the situation should never have been allowed to get out of hand in the first place.

"In my opinion," Johnson said some thirty-five years later, "Beurling's personal qualities were well known to the authorities, and he should not have been posted to 127 Wing, where teamwork was the essence, but he should have been given a long-range Mustang and been allowed to continue his lonely and personal feud against the Germans."

The public at the time was puzzled as to why the greatest Canadian fighter pilot of the war would leave operations on the eve of D day, would not be in the skies in the final push to liberate Europe. In the official announcement, Beurling himself explained his departure as a "desire to return to Canada". After all it seemed reasonable enough for the young Canadian who had given more than his share in the long, bitter struggle to return home after four years of overseas service. Canadians knew he had earned the rest. What they didn't know were the reasons it had been granted: Beurling's intractability, his continuous attacks on air-force authority, and his pathological drive to exclude himself from the pack.

The days of the eagle were numbered.

NINE

Lonely Farewell

THE HERO arrived in Halifax, May 8, 1944. Whatever his expectations, he received much less press coverage than he had had at his first homecoming sixteen months before. This time there was no question of rallies, parades, or crowds; on the contrary, the RCAF would have liked nothing better than to hide Beurling as far from civilization, and the press, as possible. The RCAF simply had no idea what to do with him. Typically, Beurling took matters into his own hands and asked for a personal interview with the Minister of Air in Ottawa, an extraordinary request for a flight lieutenant. But then, inexplicably, he just as quickly withdrew his request. Probably he had learned that the RCAF had come up with the uninspired— and uninspiring—notion of training him as a ferry pilot ("to help re-establish this officer" as the official records state), a job he knew he would loathe.

But ferry pilot he was to become, though the brass had their reservations about even this.

A memorandum from Air Vice-Marshal Curtis instructed the commanding officer at No. 3 Training Command at Saint-Hubert, Quebec, outside Montreal, that he did not consider it advisable to post Beurling "to transport work carrying passengers until he has proved himself as a steady reliable ferry pilot". Curtis was undoubtedly concerned about sending anyone up in a plane with his accident-prone ace.

Had those three crashes at Sutton Bridge and the wild plunge in the rippled Spitfire now come back to haunt Beurling? Although the official records don't mention his numerous escapes, it is naive to think that his superiors were ignorant of them. In spite of his own reservations, nevertheless, Beurling accepted the temporary assignment at Saint-Hubert.*

During the summer of 1944, No. 3 Training Command was operating what amounted to a scheduled airline service every day from Saint-Hubert to Quebec City, Mont-Joli, and Moncton. Although Beurling flew the run several times as a co-pilot on a twin-engine Beechcraft, this kind of flying could never satisfy him; it was becoming increasingly clear to him that if this was all the RCAF had to offer, then his time with them would soon be over.

Sometime in the middle of June 1944, he had a tense and strained meeting with the commanding officer of No. 3 Training Command, Air Vice-Marshal Raymond. Raymond made it clear that he was not at all pleased with his independent-minded young officer. Beurling, he felt, saw the service "only as a vehicle by which he can get his flying". For his part, Beurling told Raymond that he might very well resign and transfer to the American air force.

Five days later, Beurling formally submitted his resignation. "I feel that my services are no longer required," he wrote.

---

* Jack Scofield, one of the pilots who made several trips with Beurling, was assigned to give Beurling a refresher course in instrument flying. The "student" was put under a hood in the cockpit of a Harvard trainer and forced to manoeuvre the aircraft with his instruments alone, with no outside visual reference. Beurling dutifully carried out these exercises, Scofield says, but he clearly "couldn't wait to get the hood off and start rolls and loops".

Was Beurling told directly of the RCAF's reservations concerning his flying skills, and their concern about the safety of his passengers?

Six days after receiving Beurling's letter of resignation, Raymond advised the air force to accept it, and to transfer him to the Reserves. In the words of G. S. B. Fuller, a squadron leader and Beurling's camp commandant at No. 3, the ace was "not advantageously employable in his present rank".

On June 29, 1944, a Board of Officers convened in No. 5 Temporary Building on the shores of picturesque Dow's Lake in Ottawa. Before the day was out, the Board recommended Beurling's release from active service.

"While this officer's release will be a loss to the RCAF," the Board said, "in view of his outstanding war record every opportunity should be allowed to him to now rehabilitate himself and obtain permanent employment in civil life."

It was all over. Though it took almost six months to arrange Beurling's transfer from the RAF to the RCAF, it took only nine days for the RCAF to rid itself of him. And yet, in spite of the very real pleasure he must have felt in seeing the last of Beurling, the Chief of the Air Staff, Air Marshal Robert Leckie, produced a noble farewell on the occasion of the departure from service of Canada's most famous airman: "I wish to express to you my deep appreciation of your outstanding record in the service of your country," Leckie wrote Beurling. "Your gallant exploits and your unequalled fighting record have been a source of inspiration to all. It is only right that now having made such a splendid contribution to winning the war, approval be given to your request that you be permitted to resign your commission in order to rehabilitate yourself in civilian life."

After his resignation, the ace once again found himself in the front-page headlines; this time the press seemed

uninterested in telling the story he wanted told—the story
of his fight with the RCAF. The war was still on after all,
and it was thought unpatriotic to suggest in public that
there was a conflict between Beurling and the RCAF.

In addition, no one seemed to pay much notice when
Beurling announced he was taking steps to return to the
RAF, "the only service," he said, "in which I have been
completely happy". He told reporters that the RAF "know
how I like to work and they're quite willing to allow me to
work in that particular manner". Unhappily, the RAF did
not want him back. Two weeks before he left the RCAF,
wearing his much-decorated uniform, Beurling travelled
to New York City to try to sign up in the Army Air
Corps. This overture was without success; the Americans
were not interested either.

Finally, Beurling formally retired from the RCAF on
October 16, 1944; he left the service embittered, angry,
and unforgiving.

TEN

The Honeymoon

THE SUMMER OF 1944 found Beurling frustrated and confused. Like all Canadians, on June 6, 1944, Beurling awoke to learn of D day. All summer he was consumed by news reports of the fighting as it raged through Europe. As the Allies continued to claw their way through France, and later Holland and Germany itself, Beurling was constantly reminded of the action he was missing. He knew the Spits were back in the air, supporting the infantry with low-level strafing operations, shooting up the retreating enemy on the ground, or meeting German fighters which were poured into the front to stop the advance.

The best he could do was watch from afar. He took to holding impromptu briefings with acquaintainces in the restaurants which he frequented, especially the Chicken Coop on Ste Catherine Street in Montreal. Dozens of discarded paper napkins, bearing sketches of airplane formations and angles of deflection shooting, littered the tabletops.

This was a long and tedious summer for Beurling as he waited for his formal release from the air force and the arrival from Vancouver of Diana Gardner.

Despite the wishes of her parents, Diana had decided to move east to be close to the hero. Her mother had been against the romance since the day in May when Beurling telephoned Diana from Halifax to propose marriage.

The casual hero and the woman with impeccable taste seemed an unusual match, he from the working-class district of Verdun and she from one of Vancouver's established families.

Curiously they shared few personal interests, the least being Beurling's love of the outdoors. There was one bond, however: a mutual respect for religion. Diana followed Christian Science beliefs while George retained his faith in the teachings of the Bible. While religion was not a major factor in the romance, both respected and were aware of each other's faith and beliefs.

Compared with the slower-paced way of life on the coast, Diana found Montreal glamorous and exciting, especially the characters she was meeting in Beurling's company. They came to know Montreal's singers, dancers, and strippers. Boxers, wrestlers and their handlers too were eager to meet the hero, a man who had fought in a real fight where the stake was life or death.

Quite simply they were the toast of the town. And the social whirl into which they fell partly brought Beurling out of his shell of shyness. Leslie Roberts, who had acted as Beurling's co-author on the book *Malta Spitfire*, noticed the ace had become somewhat sophisticated.

Roberts was surprised one day when he met Beurling and Diana outside McGill Stadium after a football game to hear himself introduced to Diana as "my amanuensis".

Memories of the war nevertheless continued to haunt the hero. It is difficult to know whether the horror of Malta still played on his mind, or whether it was the thought of missing the action in France that bothered him. His favourite aunt, Dolly Murphy, said it was the former. Beurling had moved into her house in Verdun so she was able to observe him at close quarters. Dolly was struck by Beurling's inability to sleep soundly. Often that summer she would hear him leave his room in the middle of the night. When she asked where he had gone, Beurling replied, "Oh, just for a walk."

Other changes were also apparent in Beurling's lifestyle. Anyone who had flown with him, remembering his casual dress, would have been surprised at how neat he now appeared. He took to wearing conservative suits and dark ties or soft tweed jackets with a fashionable wide-brimmed fedora.

By the autumn, six weeks after resigning his commission, George and Diana were married, seven months after Beurling had proposed to her after arriving in Halifax in May.

The wedding took place on November 29, 1944, in St. George's Anglican Church in Montreal. Surprisingly, no members of either family attended the ceremony and there were no guests.

However, a friend of the Whittall family, R. O. Johnson, gave the bride away. Andy O'Brien, the Montreal newspaperman who had met Beurling in London, was best man. Beurling wore his uniform and his famous decorations for the occasion. Diana, radiant in a dark dress and wide-brimmed hat, carried a bouquet of white orchids. Following the service the couple left immediately for the Laurentians where friends had given them a chalet for the honeymoon night at the ski village of Sainte-Adèle. That night Beurling surprised the assembled guests at the nearby Sainte-Adèle Lodge by arriving alone. One of the guests at the lodge was the Canadian broadcast writer, Hugh Kemp.

"Beurling appeared on the evening of his honeymoon," Kemp says, "just wandering around with those pale, blue eyes darting everywhere. He wouldn't go to his bride and it caused quite a bit of consternation. The Sainte-Adèle Lodge was a strange little resort that attracted an odd group of expatriate royalty and aristocracy. Lady Bowater was there and a Dutch personage of royal lineage. They were a strange monied people.

"Mixed in there was this 'Billy the Kid', the gunfighter who, as the object of their attention, was respected as the killer-technician who was on our side. He wandered from cabin to cabin and I remember it was very late when he left alone walking in the snow."

The following morning Beurling hired a horse-drawn sleigh and the couple moved their luggage to the nearby chalet of one of Sainte-Adèle's most notorious residents. He was Marie Alfred Fouquereaux de Marigny. "Freddie" to his friends, de Marigny was known to the public as the man who stood accused — and later acquitted — of the murder of Sir Harry Oakes, the Canadian mining tycoon. Freddie was married to Sir Harry's eighteen-year-old daughter, Nancy, and the day after Oakes' battered body was discovered in his bed in Nassau, in the Bahamas, the son-in-law was arrested for murder. De Marigny, a twice-married Mauritian yachtsman, was lean, tall, and mysterious. Overnight he had become a sensation following his arrest in July 1943. During the trial there was evidence that shortly before the murder, Oakes and Freddie had quarrelled after the old man called him a "gigolo or worse". Freddie was set free for lack of evidence. In the late fall of 1944 he appeared at Sainte-Adèle. The details of how Beurling came to know him are lost in time. One can only speculate that Beurling must have known him well to accept an invitation to spend his honeymoon in Freddie's chalet.

Diana found it an odd experience spending their honeymoon with Freddie who shared the chalet with a woman whom "he treated like a peasant and kept in a room over the kitchen where she'd cook his meals".

At Diana's urgings, they vacated de Marigny's chalet shortly before Christmas, hiring a horse and sleigh to carry them up a nearby valley near the hamlet of Sainte-Marguerite, Quebec. There, they found a log cabin for rent which was owned by the Ferrier family. The cabin was nestled in a fairyland setting of dark spruce trees beside a small frozen pond.

The life of the valley centred on the Chalet Cochand, a ski resort two miles from the Ferrier place. The character of the valley has changed considerably since those days. Now, the hillsides are dotted with ersatz alpine bungalows, weekend retreats for wealthy Montrealers. Then, it was almost virgin woodland. Horses and sleighs brought guests from nearby Sainte-Marguerite station, the harness bells tinkling like crystal in the cold air. Except for the Hurberdeau homestead at the top of the hill above the station, the road to Chalet Cochand was devoid of houses or restaurants; only the white, lonely hills covered with black spruce, birch, and maple trees, and the stands of hardy alders guarded the passage.

Beurling loved the valley and soon he and Diana became frequent visitors to Chalet Cochand which was operated by a remarkable French-Swiss family, whose patriarch, Emile, Sr., had pioneered skiing in the district just after the turn of the century. More important to Beurling was his discovery that one of the Cochand sons, Louis, was an ex-Spitfire pilot. Louis and his brother, Emile, Jr., took an immediate liking to the young honeymoon couple. Within days of their arrival the Beurlings established a routine that seldom varied. Up before dawn, they ate breakfast cooked on a woodstove, strapped on their skis, and went cross-country through the woods to the chalet. There, Beurling took off with Emile for the higher reaches of the hill, leaving Diana, who was a poor skier, alone at the bottom, a practice which increasingly annoyed her.

Under the tutelage of Louis, Beurling would spend the

entire day perfecting his skills on the most difficult run. Louis found him intensely inquisitive about technique, the effect of gravity in turns, how to reduce wind resistance, how to increase his speed in different snow conditions, and the distribution of his weight in turns which would allow him to reduce wasted seconds, yet keep control.

"He was a perfectionist," Diana says. "He did everything over and over until he got it absolutely right." This passion for detail created a minor friction in their short marriage. "George was a great skier but I hadn't skied before so it annoyed him that I couldn't ski as well as he could. He couldn't stand inadequacies in other people."

Yet, Diana's memory of those days at Sainte-Marguerite are warm ones.

The Beurlings began entertaining the Cochand brothers in their modest log house where George often cooked; his specialty was paper-thin crêpes which he smothered in maple syrup. He also enjoyed making homemade fudge; on one occasion his zeal for fudge-making forced everyone to throw open the cabin doors and windows because the woodstove was fired up so much that the metal glowed red.

But it was the Chalet Cochand that remained the centre of their life. One evening when Diana suggested they head back to the cabin after a day's skiing, Beurling replied that he had made an arrangement with the Cochand brothers to act as a host in the chalet's cozy bar — "to be there for the guests", as he put it — in return for meals and the free use of the ski-tows. Diana never questioned his explanation and it was not until thirty years later that she discovered that no such business deal had been made (the Cochand brothers deny the story). Nevertheless, Beurling pretended to be working and haunted the lounge late every evening. Of necessity, to be near her husband, Diana frequented the lounge as well. Diana simply accepted what she thought was part of Beurling's job — entertaining guests. Dutifully she sat in the chrome-and-leather lounge until 10 p.m. before heading back on the snowy trail to the cabin and bed for an exhausted sleep.

During their time in the mountains Diana recalls that Beurling never mentioned his experiences in Malta or talked about his previous nightmares. In fact she said they "slept like logs". Emile Cochand, however, remembers once finding Beurling sitting alone in the lodge with a distant look in his eyes. When he sat down, Beurling looked up at him and said quietly, "This is the thumb that did it. . . . This is the thumb that did it." Emile knew perfectly well what the ace was referring to: pilots used the thumb of the right hand to flip the firing toggles on the Spitfire's control column. Then Beurling told Emile the details of the decapitation of the Italian pilot. "He was very quiet, and very serious," Emile said thirty-five years later.

One day in February (they had been at Sainte-Marguerite since Christmas) the pattern of their lives abruptly changed with the arrival of an eccentric New York department-store executive named Oscar Straus. Straus took an immediate liking to the war ace and his young wife. He spontaneously presented Beurling with a new Buick and the striking couple became a familiar sight, speeding along the twisting valley road.

"I remember on one occasion we were driving and George saw a plane overhead and decided to race him," Diana recalls. "We must have been going down those mountain roads at 100 m.p.h. He kept looking up and laughing. 'We're beating him. . . . We're beating him!' I was terrified. Oh, but he was marvellous."

As the spring sun crept higher each day above the mountains, Beurling, pleased with his progress on the smaller hills around Sainte-Marguerite, accepted Louis Cochand's suggestion that he might try the bigger hills at

Mont-Tremblant, farther north in the Laurentians. So, around the beginning of March 1945, they packed their bags, vacated the Ferrier's cabin, and took off in the Buick for the steeper slopes that lay beyond.

The arrival of the war ace at Mont-Tremblant created a sensation and within a few days his attention was diverted from Diana.

"He still had the women around him all the time," Diana recalls of their stay at the famous Canadian ski resort. "One day when he was off skiing up at the top of the mountain, and I was, as usual, down at the bottom, this girl came up to me and was telling me what a wonderful time she was having and that she had a date that night with George Beurling. I asked her what she did and she said she was a waitress in the lodge. I said, 'Well, I guess we'll see you at dinner' and I skied away."

Beurling's wandering eye and the attention he devoted to other women guests was painful to Diana. Also, he began spending more time alone with other skiing parties, not returning to their room until late at night. One of Beurling's favourite aprés–ski spots was a lively and informal lodge called the Manoir Pinoteau, a short distance from the main lodge at Mont-Tremblant. There, early one evening, Beurling met an attractive and exuberant young American named Vivian Stokes. It was a chance meeting, a scene that might have been set by F. Scott Fitzgerald.

On impulse the blonde American beauty had inserted a single coin in a slot machine and hit the jackpot, an ironic twist for a girl from a wealthy and privileged east-coast family. As she scooped up her winnings, she heard a man's soft voice—it was almost theatrical—asking her a question. "Do you always win?" Beurling was saying.

"Never," she laughed, "you must have brought me luck," and she turned to meet the quiet intruder; his presence she remembers was electrifying. The man stand-

ing there with the gentle smile and tanned face was dressed
entirely in black, a high turtleneck sweater and the draped
woollen ski pants of the period. Vivian Stokes says she
"was strangely disturbed by this tall, elegant figure whose
pale, haunting eyes seemed far too old for his face". They
talked only briefly, a conversation which ended with an
invitation from Beurling to meet him the following morning on the hills of Mont-Tremblant. This was the spring of
1945 when Vivian, called "Vivi" by her friends, was still in
her teens.

Vivian's late father was Sylvanus Stokes, of Richmond,
Virginia, a sportsman and sailor who had divided his time
among Virginia, Palm Beach, and Venice. Her mother
was a Fahnestock, a member of the wealthy banking family
from Massachusetts, familiar in society circles in Boston,
New York, and Newport. Vivi was born in Washington,
D.C., attended schools in England and Switzerland, and
by the time she was a teenager was fluent in French,
Italian, and German. She had been doing volunteer work
in a New York hospital that year when her mother sent
her packing to Mont-Tremblant for a skiing holiday with
her half-sister and a governess. They took over a house
near the main lodge but Vivi was bored with the formality
of Mont-Tremblant, which included dressing for dinner.
Instead, she favoured the atmosphere of Pinoteau with its
Québécois vitality and casual evening get-togethers. She
was a striking personality, best described by her cousin,
Harry Cushing: "Lusty is the name for Vivi. Her gaiety
and love of life were contagious. When you first saw her
coming at you, you imagined that the true perfect WASP
beauty was not a thing of the dreams of men, but really
existed. You were sure that this icy looking beauty was an
ideal of cool, upper-class society. But the first moment she
spoke you knew that this cool almost English accent was
liable to produce the most conventionally shocking and

intelligent sounds. Perfectly assured of her position, she decided early in life to do just what she wanted, and she wanted to live life to the fullest."

For the next few weeks Beurling and Vivi became constant companions on the ski slopes.

"He was a marvellous athlete with the grace of a panther," Vivian recalls. "He was absolutely fearless. The more dangerous the slope, the more of a challenge it was and I marvelled at his reckless, unlimited physical energy. I somehow managed to keep up, and by the end of the day I was grateful to still be in one piece. There was something about him which always made me want to try harder. Being good was not enough; I wanted to excel."

Vivi also noticed that Beurling avoided personal questions, perhaps, as she put it, "in fear of the answers". She remembers that "he seemed hungry for interesting conversation, new ideas, companionship, and he had a delightful sense of humor". Like Beurling, Vivi had married only five months before, a family-arranged marriage which was already becoming unstuck. Years later she was shocked to learn that Diana was at Mont-Tremblant during this same period, and that Beurling's marriage, like hers, had already failed.

It was a most distressing time for Diana. "They went off to ski, leaving me at the bottom of the hill. It was a great love affair. They didn't try to hide it from anyone. It was very hard for me because there wasn't anything for me to do but sit around the hotel by myself all day long."

For the record, Vivi says today, those weeks in the snow and the sun at Mont-Tremblant were platonic ones.

Painfully hurt, however, Diana concluded she had been put in the most compromising circumstances. She decided to separate and to begin divorce proceedings.

About the middle of March 1945, Beurling and Diana returned to Montreal in silence, checking into the Mount

Royal Hotel. There Diana told her husband that it was all over. "He shrugged his shoulders," she recalls. "That was his response."

Alone and unhappy, Diana decided not to return to Vancouver; she did not want to face her parents who had been against the marriage from the beginning. Instead, she travelled to Victoria; there she obained a job with the Department of Highways and moved into a rooming house. Later, she returned to Montreal to negotiate the divorce and frequently saw Beurling as a friend. Despite the disappointment of their short marriage, Diana's memory of Beurling is surprisingly warm and magnanimous. "He was a very generous man. There was nothing mean-minded in any way about him," Diana says, but adds that there was "something complex about him". Yet, while it seems a contradiction, his widow also remembers that "basically he was a very simple man, ignorant in a way, someone without much formal education who found it difficult to handle all the adulation.

"He wasn't insensitive, you know. I think in trying to get himself organized he forgot everyone else and he couldn't really understand himself.

"He was strong in the way he wanted to be a human being," Diana says. "He stood straight and strong. He was a very special person."

Shortly after Diana and Beurling separated, Vivi arrived in Montreal, taking over a private apartment, which was kept by a family friend, in the Mount Royal Hotel. The night of her arrival Beurling appeared in his uniform and they dined in a small bistro where a band played softly.

"When we danced," Vivi says, "I remember him holding me ever so gently, almost as if I were a precious Chinese vase that he was afraid might break."

As the evening progressed a friend of Beurling's joined them and offered to analyse Vivi's handwriting. She wrote the first two lines from a Marlowe poem, "Come live with me and be my Love/And we will all the pleasures prove". That evening marked the beginning of their love affair. Vivi postponed her return to New York.

Together they shared the arrival of spring, bright days that saw the warming sun turn the snow-covered streets of Montreal into currents of water. She found Beurling was a hungry reader, always borrowing books from the apartment. He took *Flight to Arras*, by Antoine de Saint-Exupéry and the latest Arthur Koestler work, *The Yogi and the Commissar*. Vivi was surprised, too, when she found that he devoured Keats and Shelley, Rupert Brooke and John Donne, but most surprising to her was his knowledge of the Bible which he could quote from memory.

With the spring snow almost gone, Vivi and Beurling decided to return to the mountains to catch the last of the skiing season.

"The skiing was quite the most difficult I had ever undertaken," she says, "but I wouldn't have admitted that to a soul."

It was during this time, too, that Vivi continued to be surprised by Beurling's gentleness and thoughtfulness.

He frequently brought her flowers, not the ordinary flower-shop variety but small bunches of wildflowers, a magical feat because spring was barely at hand. She was at a loss as to where Beurling got them and he would never tell.

Another characteristic of the man she greatly admired was his attentiveness when they were in public. Unlike some men who parade a woman on their arm, Beurling was quite the opposite. As an escort he was letter-perfect in making Vivi feel comfortable and relaxed. In her presence all Beurling's attention focused on her. In many ways, she felt, he was old-fashioned, even courtly.

When spring arrived, Vivi left for New York to make preparations to spend the summer in Mexico. As the months passed, despite their separation, their love would grow.

Unfortunately for Beurling the last spring of the war ended with tragedy. His cousin, David Murphy, the boy who played with Beurling around the old pump organ at Terrebonne, was killed fighting in Germany.

For his aunt, Dolly Murphy, it was incomprehensible that her son, the young infantryman, should die when peace was so tantalizingly close. On that April day, shortly after the news arrived of David's death, Beurling appeared at the Murphy home.

"Aunt Dolly," he said quietly, "let me take you for a drive." They got into Beurling's automobile and drove to LaSalle Boulevard, the road that follows the banks of the St. Lawrence River in Verdun and leads to the rapids of Lachine.

"George began talking about what it was like flying up there," Dolly Murphy remembers. "'You should see the colours, Aunt Dolly,' he said, 'when you fly through them. They're pink and red and blue. It is quiet, soft, and peaceful. That's where David is.'"

The words were encouraging and helpful to Dolly Murphy and she remembers it was her nephew's compassion which helped so much to ease her sorrow.

Elsewhere that spring millions of people around the world knew that the terrible sacrifices all had suffered for nearly six years were coming to an end.

The news from Germany in the first week of May 1945 was certainly the best since 1939. And the events of May 8 confirmed it.

In the dark hours of the morning, a German general was escorted into Allied headquarters in Reims, France. Alfred Jodl affixed his signature to a sheaf of documents, laid the pen on the table, and stepped back uneasily. Shortly, the official papers were on their way to Berlin where, just before midnight, the unconditional surrender of Germany was ratified at Soviet headquarters. The worst war in the history of mankind was over. Bing Coughlin's cartoon character, the woefully inept Herbie, summed up the sentiment of all Canadian servicemen when he said simply, "What I want to git most out of this war... is me!"

In Montreal, however, George Beurling was turning over in his mind a plan to get back into the war before it was Japan's turn to throw in the towel. His attention was focused on the Pacific where men were still fighting and airplanes were still flying.

ELEVEN

Dark Peace

MAY 1945 saw Beurling in Ottawa trying to re-enlist in the RCAF. Basil Dean, the columnist, bumped into him on Sparks Street where the ace told him he was trying to convince the air force to send him to the Pacific.

"We chatted for a while over a cup of coffee," Dean recalls, "but it saddened me to think of this brilliant young pilot so obviously lost in a civilian world in which his extraordinary skill had no place."

The RCAF went through the motions with Beurling's request but quickly rejected it.

Air Vice-Marshal H. L. Campbell reported in an official memorandum that Beurling "called at headquarters in Ottawa stating he was extremely anxious to serve on operation in the Pacific Theatre". Campbell's reaction was negative. "From a view of this officer's file," he wrote, "it would be obvious that he would not be suitable as a regular officer in the RCAF, and therefore, it is not considered that he should be appointed to a commission in the RCAF at this time."

A higher authority agreed. The new Minister of Air, Colin W. G. Gibson, scrawled one word on Campbell's memo above his stamp of office — "Concur".

Beurling's record, his skirmishes with authority, and the incidents of his turbulent service with 127 Wing in England, was on file and fresh in the minds of the official air force; his rejection should come as no surprise. While Beurling waited for a decision from the RCAF, he also approached the Chinese legation in Ottawa, offering his services for the Chinese National Air Force. Beurling confessed he was turned down as well by the Chinese, although he never explained why.

The press continued to report his movements but on a smaller scale. He was inside-page material now. The big news was in the Pacific where the grim events of Nagasaki and Hiroshima got the biggest headlines of all. The world was weary of war, perhaps even of heroes, and as the summer ended the first Canadian serviceman began arriving home.

Some years before, the official machinery had been put into motion to absorb Canada's returning warriors. On December 8, 1939, an Order-in-Council had authorized the establishment of fourteen government sub-committees to pave the way for demobilization; these sub-committees would deal with employment, loans, housing, war gratuities, and education. From 1946 to 1950 veterans' rehabilitation took more taxpayers' dollars than any other national expense. No one complained; there was an enormous debt to be paid.

Overnight, the pages of the country's telephone directories told the story under the letter "V". There were veterans' taxi companies, veterans' dry cleaners, veterans' cafés, veterans' garages — on and on the list went. Suburban orchards echoed to the sound of bulldozers and carpenters' hammers. Love blossomed and its effects would cause nightmares for every schoolboard in the country in the 1950s.

The vets themselves poured back to school by the tens of thousands. In 1947, university enrolment peaked at 37,000. The veterans were everywhere.

George Beurling, the country's best-known veteran,

was entitled to any number of benefits as a comrade-in-arms. Strangely, he asked for nothing except to take his War Service Gratuity which amounted to $1,143.28 — by no means a king's ransom but enough to help him start down the road of peace. The records of the Department of Pensions and National Health contain only one letter from Beurling, reminding the bureaucrats in Ottawa to hasten payment of his gratuities "as I have been counting on this money".

His mustering-out pay kept him going until October 1945, when he joined the Sun Life Assurance Company in Montreal as a life underwriter, working out of the company's St. James Street branch. On December 27 he resigned, having not sold a single policy.

The new year saw him restless and unsettled, afflicted with a purposelessness that brought attention to itself in a strange way. One evening he had gone to one of his favourite spots, the Normandy Roof of Montreal's Mount Royal Hotel, where part of the dinner entertainment included an appearance by the graphologist Jacquemain, who analysed the handwriting of the guests. Beurling wrote a sample, signed a false name, and passed the note to the so-called graphologist through a companion. He waited nervously for her interpretation.

Slowly Jacquemain delivered her verdict. "The person who wrote this," she said, "has no aim in life."

Jacquemain's assessment may have been unfair. Beurling had told a Montreal newspaperman, Ken Johnstone, that his failure to get a civilian flying job was frustrating. "I certainly didn't grow up with the idea of shooting down people," he told Johnstone bitterly. "It was a job that had to be done." He complained that he had "tackled every flying concern in Canada from TCA and CPA down but that the answer was always the same: 'We can't use fighter pilots.'" However, both airlines today deny that

Beurling ever tried to get a job with them.

Ron Keith, director of public relations for CP Air, notes that there is no record "of approach to Mr. Beurling by CPA or of any application he may have made to us for employment".

G. G. "Gaff" Edward, a senior Air Canada pilot who, from 1945 to 1970, was involved with nearly every pilot that Air Canada hired, says there is "no record of Beurling ever showing any interest in us, and as far as I can remember, we never courted him". Edward adds that while Air Canada hired a few fighter pilots, the airline was more interested in pilots with experience on multi-engine aircraft.

It is difficult to trace Beurling's movements in the years following war's end. He told reporters of different flying jobs he had had as a freelancer, but with so many postwar flying companies springing up, and just as quickly disappearing, it is impossible to trace records. Beurling also spoke of going to Hollywood with Freddie de Marigny for a screen test. A survey of the major studios has failed to produce any evidence to substantiate his claim. He talked, too, of a flying deal in the Bahamas, but like so many of his claims the details are too vague for a thorough examination.

Beurling did work briefly from May until October in 1947 as an instructor for Sherbrooke Airways, in Sherbrooke, Quebec.

That same autumn he appeared at the Cape Breton Flying Club in Nova Scotia where he purchased one of the club's War Assets Tiger Moths for $1,000. Beurling flew the Moth, registration number CF-BSX, back to Montreal, where he kept it in a farmer's field at Terrebonne.

There, we get a rather sad portrait of the famous ace attempting to generate revenue by selling rides to the locals at a nearby racetrack. First, he had to play down his image as the reckless, devil-may-care fighter pilot. His brother, David, says quite frankly, "The local populace was leery of flying with him." To attract customers, Beurling used his kid brother to shame them into paying for a ride. With a five-dollar bill which George had given him, David would appear in the crowds and in a loud voice say, "Mister, can I go for a ride?" Beurling would take David for a spin. Returning to the racetrack, the brothers hoped that the local girls would have persuaded their boyfriends to follow the example of a ten-year-old who showed no reservation about flying with the ex-ace. Beurling's efforts to earn money this way, although harmless, seem inappropriate for the country's great hero.

David, who today holds a pilot's licence, firmly rejects any suggestion that George was a reckless flier. David remembers once seeing his brother surveying the ground the day before he was to perform some stunts, which included flying between two telephone poles. He carefully measured the distance between the poles and the height from the ground to the wires, and he studied the prevailing winds. David remembers him as a perfectionist, a description that the few people who were close to Beurling frequently use to describe the lanky pilot.

It is doubtful whether his one-man flying circus generated enough cash to be profitable. In the brief period that Beurling owned the Moth, however, he managed to get himself in hot water with the Department of Transport for taking passengers for hire, a practice for which he wasn't licensed; soon he was the subject of an RCMP investigation. No charges were brought against him because, as Inspector P. S. Walker of the Air Regulations Branch of DOT, recorded, "Reports are rather inconclusive and it would appear to be difficult to take any action on the information gathered so far by the RCMP."

Beurling was also under federal scrutiny for allowing

his limited commercial pilot's certificate to expire. Further, while flying with Sherbrooke Airways, he had violated regulations twice that summer for "flying in weather below VFR [visual flight rules] limits".

Whether Beurling was having more problems than other returned veterans is debatable. His failure to adjust to peacetime Canada was complicated by his continuing desire to fly. He told *Maclean's* magazine writer John Clare he found it incomprehensible that so many of his former wingmates could give up a life of flying for less exciting pursuits and referred to ex-wingmates who had taken up commercial flying as a "bunch of truck drivers".

In the spring of 1947, at the urging of her family, Diana agreed to begin divorce proceedings which she reasoned would be more effectively done in Montreal. So she left her job in Victoria and returned east to begin the process which in those days involved a circuitous route through the Senate of Canada. Diana and Beurling saw each other for the occasional date at the movies or dinner. She was determined, nevertheless, to make a clean break with Beurling and there was no talk of reconciliation. Besides he had continued to see Vivi Stokes who travelled often to Montreal, despite her busy schedule. She was modelling, doing research for a political columnist in New York, and going through the motions of getting her own divorce. As 1947 came to a close Vivian was back in Canada for another rendezvous with Beurling. It was something both had planned and looked forward to for some months, a flight in Beurling's Moth to a remote retreat north of Montreal. They flew for several hours before Beurling banked for a gentle landing on a snow-covered lake. The setting was idyllic, Vivi recalls, isolated and quiet. They stayed at a fishing lodge which had been closed for the winter. Beurling had made arrangements with the owner to use one of the camp's small log cabins.

The New York society girl was delighted with the simplicity of the place. They had flown in provisions, including skis, and over the next few days explored the shoreline and many of the trails that wound through the pines. They chopped wood for the fireplace and stove and at twilight cooked dinner. Beurling was amused by Vivi's concern over wild animals and kidded her in a good-natured way. Vivi says she had never seen him in such a relaxed, contented mood, satisfied simply to sit and read. He talked about Saint-Exupéry, telling Vivi that, of all the writers he had read on the subject of flying, Saint-Exupéry came closest to describing what it was really like to be alone in the sky.

"Late one evening," she remembers, "I had been reading to him, either Saint-Exupéry or Masters' *Spoon River Anthology*, but I had to stop. The fire was almost out, only a few smoldering embers remained, and I remember moonlight creeping through the windows. I had never seen him more relaxed or happy, and he was extremely tender during these intimate moments and held me close to him for a long time."

A week later, they put out the fires, cranked up the airplane, and took off from the frozen lake in a rush of snow and wind. They had promised to see each other more often. Vivi went back to New York, Beurling to his favourite haunts in Montreal.

There is, however, a conflicting view of Beurling's state of mind as the year came to a close. Diana found him more bitter than Vivi had described. Sometimes, Diana said, he waited outside the CBC office where she now worked, occasionally borrowing money. Diana also said he appeared to be somewhat threadbare and on one very cold day noticed that "he didn't even have a pair of gloves".

Still, Beurling continued to play the role of man about town, a familiar figure in some of Montreal's more popular nightclubs and restaurants. It is difficult to imagine how someone could spend so much time in restaurants, bars, and nightclubs and still abstain from alcohol. Beurling did it by sticking to soft drinks served on the rocks in highball glasses. In 1948 he told Frank Hamilton of *New Liberty* magazine not to believe the stories that he had been "seen drunk as a lord". Beurling told the reporter he was drinking as many as fifty Coca-Colas a day!

The Chicken Coop was still one of his favourite restaurants, and Diana sometimes joined him for coffee as he doodled on paper napkins, invariably drawing diagrams of the angle of a deflection shot. In her recollection, Beurling seemed to be a parody of himself, the famous veteran who couldn't forget the experience of war and was still gripped by its awful power.

The country was now into its third year of peace and for more and more veterans the war seemed long over. Thousands of young men were still in university, many trying to find an easy way to juggle the demands of their studies with those of raising a family.

Before 1947 passed into history, an event took place which was to give some direction to the life of the Canadian war hero. One Saturday afternoon towards the end of November, with the snow already deep in the Laurentians, delegates to the General Assembly of the United Nations voted to partition Palestine. Beurling, whether or not he was aware of the historic vote, would find purpose in the conflict that everyone knew would follow that fateful announcement.

TWELVE

The Machal

IN PALESTINE, word of the partition was greeted with violence. Angry Arabs in Jerusalem reacted to the news by burning down the city's commercial centre which was made up of a cluster of Jewish shops. The same evening three Jews were ambushed and killed outside of Tel Aviv. Unlike most impending wars in history, everyone knew exactly when this one was going to begin. The British Mandate in Palestine would terminate May 14, 1948. For the Haganah, the underground Jewish Army, there was no time to lose. Its members were fanning out across the world, racing against the clock to complete their assignment: to beg, borrow, or buy the tools of battle. For the moment, 100,000 British troops stood between the Arabs and the Jews of Palestine, but as the date of the British withdrawal drew nearer, terrorism mounted on both sides. Bombings and shootings erupted in every corner of the Holy Land and the world watched with apprehension.

Very quickly, too, the Haganah realized the dimension that the conflict would take. This was not going to be a war where men answered the call to arms with handguns they had hidden under the floorboards in their homes. The Jews faced overwhelming tactical odds; the Arab armies were equipped with artillery, tanks, and aircraft, modern firepower that would have to be met in kind. The Jews were desperately short of everything, but no shortage was quite as critical as the lack of trained combat pilots. Because there were so few pilots and aircraft, they would have to go abroad for both. North America offered the biggest pool of wartime airmen and it was here that the search began. The recruiters themselves were either American or Canadian Jews dedicated to preserving the emerging state of Israel, men who were prepared to go to any length to see the state protected. They held no rank and received no pay; their secret organization bore no name. Their task was a singular one: to gather the arms of war and to seek volunteers to fight in the service of the Jews. These recruits were to become known in Hebrew as the "Machal", an acronym for "Mitnadvei Hutz Laa'retz" —"volunteers from abroad".

One American recruiter, Sidney Mandel, was responsible for interviewing candidates in the enormous area that stretched from the Canadian border in the north to Texas in the south, east as far as Cleveland and west to Denver. Moving like a phantom, Mandel crisscrossed half a continent in his search for recruits.

In Canada the clandestine recruiters concentrated their efforts in three of the country's major population centres: Montreal, Toronto, and Vancouver. In the search for Canadian pilots, none was as qualified as a thirty-two-year-old Montreal printing executive named Sydney Shulemson. He was an expert pilot who became the most decorated Jewish-Canadian serviceman of the war. Flying out of Scotland, he had roamed the North Sea as the leader of a strike wing in Coastal Command, hunting and destroying German convoys sneaking along the Norwegian coast. Shulemson's pleasant manners belied his fearsome war record which had won him the Distinguished Service Order and the Distinguished Flying Cross.

Shulemson was one of five Canadian Jews in Montreal who had undertaken the task of secret recruiting and arms purchases, an endeavour which raised potentially serious legal problems as Canadian law prohibited recruiting of Canadian citizens by foreign governments. Fortunately, since there was as yet no formal State of Israel, the legality of recruiting remained moot. But to be on the safe side, Shulemson and his nameless organization went underground. As far as he was concerned, what the group was doing was outside the law.

"While the government was not discouraging us too strenuously," Shulemson says, "what we were doing in the way of recruiting personnel and gathering materiel for military purposes was illegal. I had the distinct impression that we were under pretty careful surveillance."

The Montreal group took the most cautious measures to escape detection. The members kept no written records, and most telephone calls were made through public pay phones. Meetings were held in cars or in noisy restaurants. In the case of three of the group of five, who were reserve officers, the safest meeting place was a most obvious one, the officers' mess of the Royal Canadian Corps of Signals located in an armoury on Bleury Street. Over regimental silver and crystal, Shulemson plotted the purchase of materiel and the recruiting of men for the beleaguered Jews of Palestine.

The most obvious source of recruits came from the ranks of Jewish–Canadian veterans, of whom there were over 20,000. Using the Canadian Jewish Congress as an umbrella, Shulemson found the organization an effective vehicle to make his plea for volunteers.

"We had sent out letters to all the Jewish veterans of Montreal and Toronto. We called public meetings, not for the purpose of recruiting staff, that was not in the letter, but we explained that we were concerned about the safety of Israel. The meetings were usually held in a synagogue and we had very careful security control so that only

Jewish boys who were known veterans and could be vouched for were admitted to the meetings."

All told, more than 300 volunteers would come from this reserve of Canadian war veterans.

The first indication that Canada's foremost war hero might be interested in joining the Machal's ranks came one snowy January afternoon in the bar of Nymark's ski lodge at Saint-Sauveur-des-Monts in the Laurentians. Shulemson, an avid downhill and cross-country skier, had retired to the noisy bar for a quiet drink after a strenuous day on the slopes. Sitting at a nearby table was one of his confrères from the group of five. Suddenly the man made his way across the room and joined Shulemson at his table.

"Beurling is anxious to meet you," the man said.

"Does he know me?" Shulemson asked nonchalantly.

"No. He doesn't know who you are or what you do." Shulemson took a sip of his drink, his twinkling blue eyes surveying the crowded lounge. A few tables away George Beurling was sitting and laughing with a group of men and women.

"Well," Shulemson replied, "I'm not ready to meet him."

For good reason. Beurling had already been quoted in the local press as saying that he had been approached by several Arab governments to consider offers to fly on the Arab side. Around the Montreal Press Club the figure of $5,000 a month was being bandied about as the amount Beurling had been offered. When Shulemson heard the stories his interest in Beurling had faded rapidly. The last person the Machal wanted was a mercenary. The Machal recruiters were primarily looking for men with an ideological commitment to the cause. Second, there was no money to hire pilots. This is not to say that some Machal pilots did not receive mercenary pay; in a few cases, volunteers were paid substantial amounts. Since

Machal recruiters across the country were for the most part wealthy and influential members of the local Jewish communities, some of them made private financial arrangements with a recruit which usually took the form of a promise to deposit certain monies into the bank account of the person they had engaged. The funds would be collected from Jews in the local community. Nevertheless, it was not a practice which Shulemson and his recruiters followed.

To this day Beurling's motives in approaching the Jews remain partly in doubt. One of the many people with whom Beurling talked of his plans that winter of 1948 was another ex-Spitfire ace, Rod Smith, who like Beurling had fought in Malta, and who had later served at Biggin Hill although in a different squadron. Beurling had tried to persuade Smith to fight for the Arabs for $1,600 a month.

"I told him," Smith says, "that I didn't know what the war there was all about, and that I wanted to finish university. I couldn't bring myself to tell him you should never shoot at anyone for money, because I was sure it was not Arab money, and I knew it was not Zionist zeal, that attracted him to Palestine. He had always tended to be unstable in all things outside of flying and shooting and because of this, much of what he said could not be taken literally."

As spring approached, Beurling's persistent pleas to members of the Jewish community in Montreal prompted Shulemson to seek advice from his counterpart in New York. Using the code name "Canadian Tiger" for Beurling, Shulemson contacted the Haganah in New York for their reaction. Shortly, the word came back: he was to proceed with a preliminary meeting but make no commitment.

The face-to-face meeting with Beurling took place a short time later in a private home in Montreal's fashionable Westmount, a community of tree-lined streets and expensive homes. Although Shulemson had seen Beurling several times around town and in the mountains, it had always been at a distance. Now that they sat together a few feet apart, Shulemson could not escape those penetrating blue eyes. He also was struck by Beurling's easy grace of movement.

"We're not hiring mercenaries," Shulemson began.

"I'm not a mercenary," Beurling replied.

"You won't go hungry," Shulemson continued. "You'll have money for cigarettes and that type of thing. But no pay."

"Well, I'm interested," Beurling said.

Drawing on his knowledge of the Scriptures, Beurling explained that, to him, the Jews of Palestine had a justifiable claim on Israel. His explanation so surprised Shulemson that he could only conclude that "some compelling motive within him superseded his desire for money and publicity".

Shulemson felt so positive about these feelings of Beurling's that he arranged to meet with him several more times. Beurling's sense of conviction seemed absolutely genuine; even more surprisingly the sentiments he was expressing were not those Shulemson had been reading in the local press.

At another meeting, this one held sometime in March 1948, in a room in the Mount Royal Hotel, Beurling met another Canadian Jew who was also recruiting for the Machal. This was the fiercely handsome Ben Dunkelman who, like Shulemson, was a distinguished Canadian war veteran. The son of a prominent Jewish family, owners of the large clothing concern Tip Top Tailors, Dunkelman had joined the Queen's Own Rifles as a recruit. By the time the war had ended, Dunkelman had risen to the rank of major and had won the DSO. As an infantry officer, he had fought his way from the beaches of Normandy across France, Belgium, and Holland.

"Beurling was a very handsome young man," Dunkelman says. "He was striking in appearance. He had these very unusual eyes. I remember that impressing me. He had a strong look about him, a very determined look. I knew of his fabulous reputation as a fighter but I was very careful in screening everyone." Dunkelman adds, however, that he was skeptical of everyone's motives who was offering his services.

"I wanted to make sure of Beurling, and in a lengthy discussion I tried to discourage him in every way. I told him we couldn't offer any specific pay. There would be no glamour. We didn't even have uniforms. Also, as far as I knew, we had no planes to fly as yet, and that even food was a great problem to us. I was acutely aware of that because some of the money I had raised to buy arms and ammunition was taken away to buy wheat."

During the discussion, Beurling claimed he was not "the least bit interested in money". At this point, Dunkelman remembers, the Canadian ace pulled out several letters from his pocket and handed them to him. "I've had many offers," Beurling said.

Those letters contained offers of a job as a mercenary pilot in South America. After Dunkelman returned the letters, he levelled his eyes on Beurling. "Why," he asked, "are you so interested in helping us?"

"You people have been without a state for thousands of years, wandering homeless and persecuted," Beurling replied. "I would be helping to fulfill the prophecies and teachings of the Bible." Dunkelman says the words are vivid in his memory.

The meeting ended with Dunkelman endorsing Beurling, convinced of the sincerety of his motives as a volunteer for the Machal. Shulemson conveyed their impressions to the Haganah in New York and waited.

Characteristically, while Beurling waited for word of approval, he plunged into the adventure with his usual vigour, devising a number of outlandish cloak-and-dagger plans which he submitted to Shulemson for approval.

In one of these, Beurling and twelve other pilots would be secretly sent to Cyprus where they would lead a raid on a Spitfire squadron based there. They would neutralize the guard, steal all the aircraft of an entire squadron, and fly them to Israel.

A second and equally dangerous plot involved Beurling joining the Arab air force and defecting to the Jews with what would have then been Israel's only Spitfire.

The third, and most bizarre proposal, involved a report that Beurling had been killed in a flying accident. This would give Beurling a tactical advantage, he reasoned, for if the Arabs believed he was out of action, they would be less vigilant on patrols. He'd knock down a couple of planes, he said, before they would know he was there.

Though Shulemson felt the schemes were all too risky, he still consulted his superiors in New York, who predictably rejected them. On the other hand they instructed Shulemson to sign Beurling on. Wisely, for reasons of security, Shulemson withheld the news from the ace until the Machal was actually ready to feed the Canadian Tiger into the Palestine pipeline. Other volunteers were already being given their marching orders, including Dunkelman whose special talent as a heavy-mortars officer was soon going to be in urgent demand. He suddenly left for Palestine.

Yet, despite Shulemson's rigid security measures in dealing with Beurling, the Machal recruiter was startled to discover that his prize pilot had already gone to the press. "He had made an arrangement with one of the newspapermen in the city to give him the story," Shulemson says.

What Shulemson didn't know was that not only had Beurling gone to a local news reporter, but he was also holding interviews with perhaps as many as half-a-dozen journalists, including two writers from Canada's very popular monthly magazines, *Maclean's* and *New Liberty*. Further, he had made a deal with the Montreal *Standard* to be a war correspondent in Palestine. Dozens if not hundreds of Montrealers knew of Beurling's imminent departure.

Naturally, one of the very first to hear the news was Vivi Stokes. During the period after their Laurentian interlude the previous November, the society girl and Beurling had become closer than ever. Her visits to Montreal had grown more frequent, and Beurling often travelled to see her in New York.

One aspect of the intense relationship was that it left each partner completely independent of the other. Never did one demand explanations of the other's actions. It was this respect for each other's privacy that in a strange way brought the two free spirits inextricably closer. When Beurling told her of his dramatic plans, Vivi felt compelled to ask him his reasons for going to Israel although she knew the question was an intrusion.

"I'm going to be incredibly wealthy," Beurling replied, quietly without hesitation.

His reply left her surprised and bewildered. During Beurling's sojourns in New York there was never any suggestion in her mind that he had reason to be preoccupied with greatly improving his fortune. On the contrary, on those New York visits, he appeared impeccably dressed in a fashionably cut grey-flannel suit and quiet tie that belied the shabby image of an unemployed pilot. They dined well, if not lavishly, and there was never a hint in Beurling's manner or actions that he was down on his luck. Vivi remembers her escort always had money to pay a restaurant bill or to buy flowers, a book, or a record. However, it never occurred to the wealthy American aristocrat to wonder where the money came from. Beurling's remark that his contract to fly with the Israelis was inspired by avarice has continued to haunt Vivi Stokes since that tragic spring of 1948. She has frequently wondered whether Beurling felt it necessary to match her lifestyle. The thought is a most disturbing one for Vivi. If it was true had she directly contributed to his death? It remains for her a tormenting question, one for which she has never found a comfortable answer. The truth about their relationship had certainly become clear to both; they were desperately in love. And it was only a short time before Beurling left for the Middle East that he presented Vivi with a gold band. Inscribed inside were the initials "GFB–VS" and the words from the Lord's Prayer "Forever and ever". When Vivi, a left-hander, put the ring on her right hand, Beurling removed it, fitted the band on Vivi's left hand, and said quietly, "You'll have to get used to wearing it there." Vivi did not protest.

Others besides Vivi have wondered about the "money" question: was Beurling a mercenary, or did he only claim to be one? His motives for going to Palestine raise more questions than they answer. On the one hand he was telling Smith, the ex-Malta pilot, and others of the enormous pay he had been offered by the Arabs. On the other hand, while he continued to express in public mercenary greed, there is no doubt in either Sydney Shulemson's or Ben Dunkelman's mind that Beurling did not volunteer for the Machal for pay. They are adamant that no money was offered or paid to Beurling for his services.

Equally confusing were Beurling's remarks to John Clare who, in preparing his article for *Maclean's*, quoted

Beurling leaves Buckingham Palace after being decorated by
King George VI. The woman on the left is Jean Johnson, a
Red Cross nurse from Cleveland, Ohio.

A borrowed hat under his arm, Beurling is sworn into the
RCAF on September 1, 1943, at RCAF Headquarters in
London.

Hugh Godefroy grounded Beurling for low flying in the fall
of 1943.

Unidentified fitters pose with Beurling's Spitfire at 412
Squadron base, Biggin Hill, Kent, in November 1943.
The plane, a Mark IXb, carries $30\frac{1}{3}$ kills denoted by the
swastikas on the fuselage. The ace would claim one more kill.
The RCAF credited him with an official total of $29\frac{1}{3}$.

Beurling (*right*), F. O. Stan Payne (*centre*), and Freddie
Murray (*left*), wingmates from 412 Squadron, pose in front
of two Mark IXb Spitfires at Biggin Hill in November 1943.

Beurling and Diana on their wedding day, November 29, 1944.

Photo–Canada Wide

Photographers loved to pose Beurling with pretty girls.
This is Dorothy Rice who sent kiss-autographed photos to
10,000 Canadian servicemen.

Beurling (*right*), out of
uniform at the Sainte-Adèle,
Quebec, annual horse show.

Vivi Stokes, age nineteen.

The Norseman burns at Urbe Airport, outside Rome, on
May 20, 1948.

Italian Jews mourn with the Chief Rabbi of Rome
around the simple casket.

Hundreds of Romans joined the funeral procession five days after the fatal air crash. Two black horses pulled the casket through the streets of Rome to Verano Cemetery.

For two years Beurling lay buried in Rome's Protestant cemetery near the graves of Keats and Shelley.

Foreign volunteers in Israel's War of Independence are honoured in this memorial. Beurling's name is spelled "Burling".

A hero's grave near Mount Carmel, Israel.

Beurling as saying, "I know it may sound hard, but I will drop bombs or fire guns from a plane for anyone who will pay me" and that he would fly "for the one who will pay the most".

Who was paying him? Where did the money come from? There are no simple answers. Was he being paid by the Arabs and flying for the Israelis? It is a question that Vivi Stokes, too, has asked. Not long before Beurling left for Israel, she mentioned in casual conversation that she too might be in the Middle East that summer; she might accept an invitation from her cousin, Summerville Pinkney Tuck, the U.S. Ambassador to Egypt, to visit him in Cairo.

"Let me know if you go," Beurling replied. "I have friends there."

In later years Vivi entertained the possibility that Beurling was a double agent, in the pay of the British while flying for the Israelis. She recalls Beurling's constant references to Britain, the RAF, and the British Empire. Instinctively she sensed a deep commitment and loyalty on Beurling's part to Great Britain.

Although she never pursued the subject in conversation, Vivi, after so many years, still cannot shake from her mind the possibility that Beurling was in the service of British intelligence. In the crazy world of international espionage, how simple it would have been for the British to employ Beurling, using his mercenary image as the perfect cover.

Or was Beurling no more than he appeared to be, a man who found postwar Canada utterly dull? Rod Smith reasoned it was only that. "He was someone who could not fit in anywhere in peacetime," his fellow ace concluded. "I think he just wanted to go blindly back to the milieu where he had shone."

It is a view that his widow, Diana, shares too. "He had

been terribly disillusioned with the broken promises," she said of Beurling's decision to go to Palestine. "He was very bitter about his country and saddened by his experiences. At the end he really wanted to get out of Montreal and out of the country."

By May 1948, that journey had begun. In Palestine, the political time bomb was ticking away. Everyone knew it would go off on May 14, the day the British mandate expired. On Saturday, May 1, Sydney Shulemson got the word to send the Canadian Tiger into battle, an order that was simply executed by telephone.

"Will you meet me for lunch?" Shulemson asked.

"Fine. Where?" Beurling said.

"At the Mount Royal," Shulemson instructed him, adding, "and bring your passport. I want to check it."

At noon, Beurling wandered into the lobby of the popular Montreal hotel where Shulemson was waiting.

"I just walked him right out of the lobby into my car," Shulemson says. "I drove him to the airport and bought him a ticket for New York. He didn't even have a toothbrush with him when he left Montreal."

Beurling may have sensed he was about to leave. A few days before, he had dined with Diana at the Chicken Coop. When it was time to go, he walked her to a taxicab, put her inside, and leaned inside towards the driver.

"Take care of this lady, cabbie," Beurling said, "She's my wife."

Then Diana turned and looked into those extraordinary eyes and saw that he was crying.

Death on the Tiber

THE MOOD IN MANHATTAN contrasted sharply with the news of an imminent war in the Middle East. New York was enjoying the postwar years with an exuberance that it had not known for a decade. Gone were the khaki uniforms of the war years, replaced by brighter colours of the men's sport coats and the women's dresses. Everyone was reading *Tales of the South Pacific* by James Michener, listening to Edward R. Murrow, and watching a new novelty called television. New Yorkers were lining up to get into the fashionable Stork Club.

On the first day of May in 1948 a Yellow taxicab was hurtling through the streets of Manhattan to the Henry Hudson Hotel. The passenger was George Beurling, the pilot-pilgrim on his way to the Holy Land, oblivious to the frantic life about him. He was one of a handful of ex-pilots from the Second World War who were also on the move that day from Panama City to Miami, from El Paso to Paris.

In an exercise that could in no way involve written orders, the Haganah and Machal recruiters, such as Shulemson in Montreal and Mandel in Chicago, were managing to feed their recruits into an underground pipeline that would eventually bring them to Israel. In addition to directing pilots to their secret rendezvous points, the Jewish agents were also arranging for the flow of arms and ammunition across oceans and selected borders.

In various stages of transit were rifles, machine guns, anti-aircraft guns, shells, helmets, empty sandbags, even mosquito nets, penicillin, and salt tablets. By subterfuge and cunning, bribery and gall, men and materiel were finding their way to the shores of Israel. Hiding a shipment of salt pills was relatively easy, but flying a four-engine Constellation, a Flying Fortress, or a Mustang fighter out of some airport in New Jersey or Florida demanded imagination and invention. In fact, with a U.S. arms embargo in effect, the mission seemed impossible.

The job of procuring aircraft for the new state fell to a small flying outfit called the Aviron Company. The deals it made were the first steps towards the creation of the fledgling Israeli air force, then called "Sherut Avir"—"Air Service"—which, until the day of independence, operated illegally and secretly. Aviron went to great lengths to carry out its purchasing assignments, including in one instance forming a fake movie company to get four surplus Beaufighters out of England to Israel. In addition, Aviron made deals at steep if not exorbitant prices with private charter companies to transport arms and ammunition. The carriers got their money up front and asked no questions.

One cover operation was established in Spain. In early 1948, while George Beurling waiting in Montreal to meet the Machal recruiters, a group of Jewish agents feverishly put together a ghost airline company in Madrid. The U.S. air force had suddenly declared surplus fifty of its C-64 light-cargo aircraft. Because the planes could not be purchased for military purposes, the company in Spain purchased twenty C-64's as commercial freighters.

The aircraft Americans called the C-64 was known to every Canadian bushpilot in the late 1930s as the Norseman, the creation of the brilliant Dutch designer Robert Noorduyn.

The Norseman was the classic Canadian bushplane. It was versatile and rugged and, carrying the same amount of fuel as its competitors, it could take a bigger payload a little further. The prototype was flown in mid–November 1935 and, by the time the war ended, over 1,500 Norsemans had rolled off the assembly line. Over 759 saw service in the U.S. air force and army during the Second World War.

The plane was powered by a single Pratt and Whitney nine-cylinder air-cooled radial engine, the same power plant used in the Harvard trainers that had become the mainstay in the British Commonwealth Air Training Plan. Fitted in a Norseman, the combination made the aircraft a perfect powerful light-transport plane. The Norseman was not a demanding aircraft to fly. The fabric covering made its controls relatively heavy and it was slow to respond. It was simply reliable, an airplane that always got you there and back. Curiously, while it was designed by a Dutchman, it somehow reflected a Canadian personality; it was strong and dependable, not in the least exotic, but unglamorously functional.

By the time Beurling reached New York to wait for his next travel orders, the legally incorporated but fake Spanish company began taking delivery of its fleet of twenty Norseman airplanes. From points throughout Europe the planes made their way to Nice, France, the first leg of a long journey that it was hoped would end in Israel. One of the planes bore the tail number N69822.

Beurling, meanwhile, after checking into the Henry Hudson, left his room and walked the short distance to Vivi Stokes' apartment on West 55th Street. Vivi's comfortable, sunlit flat was located just off Fifth Avenue, a quiet hideaway high above the din of Manhattan. Here the couple was sealed from the outside world. It was in this apartment that Vivi and Bunny—her nickname for Beurling—idled away the hours, reading and listening to music, particularly the works of Mozart and Puccini. In the bookcases that lined Vivi's walls there was always a new book to savour. The next three days, the last the couple would spend together, were measured in seconds.

"If I had any previous commitments," Vivi says, "either business or social, they were cancelled. He made it quite clear that he just wanted to be with me."

Vivi also spent a lot of time giving Beurling Italian lessons, a language which he had begun studying shortly after meeting her. To get the accent right, Beurling sang along with recordings of Italian opera.

At Vivi's apartment they talked long into the night, of camping and skiing in Quebec and of Rome, for the Machal had told Beurling that was to be his next stop on the road to Palestine. Vivi noticed that Beurling seemed pleased to be "starting a new life far away, getting a small apartment and using that as a base". But she noticed, too, that he seemed somehow troubled but she refrained from interrupting his thoughts with questions. Occasionally he made telephone calls that attracted her attention by their abruptness, conversations that consisted of "Hello. . . . Yes. . . . No. . . ". These conversations would often leave him silent and withdrawn.

On May 3, 1948, a Monday, Beurling got his departure orders. That night, their last together, Beurling and Vivi spent the hours quietly.

"We had dinner at a small French bistro on West 56th Street between 5th and 6th avenues called Chez George," Vivi says of that farewell evening. Later, they strolled to Broadway, looking for an amusement hall they had seen on previous walks.

"There were all sorts of funny games, pinball machines

and a shooting gallery where one aimed at little plastic ducks moving along on a trolley," Vivi remembers. "Of course he beat me at that too, and won a horrid little furry monkey which dangled on an elastic string, the sort of gadget a travelling salesman sticks in his automobile. He gave it to me to carry and we went on to have one of those funny photographs taken. There was only one copy and he took it with him.

"We walked back to my apartment and talked again of Rome. From the conversation I gathered that money would be coming in, and for the first time I felt this meant something to him," Vivi says. Yet she didn't explore the topic further.

That evening, too, Vivi wore the gold ring Beurling had given her. She had placed it back on her right hand, and again Beurling asked her to wear it on her left.

"To please him," Vivi says, "I changed the ring and he looked at my hand and said, 'Remember. Sooner or later, you're going to have to get used to it.'"

In the morning they walked the short distance to the Henry Hudson Hotel, where Vivi wanted to help him pack. "I was amazed that he only had one small suitcase," she says, "the size one would take for a weekend." As she packed, Vivi gave Beurling a small St. Christopher medal, one she remembers was no larger than a nickel. On the back she had the words engraved, "Please do nothing dangerous". Beurling studied the medal, smiled, and put it in his wallet.

"I put his few things in order and stuck the small monkey in the corner of the suitcase," Vivi continued. "Even though we were planning to see each other within a month, I was strangely upset that I couldn't go to the airport with him but I did not ask why. Just before I left, he put his arms around me, kissed me goodbye, and my last words to him were, 'God bless you, Bunny.'"

In the lobby, Vivi silently watched as Beurling checked out and called for his valuables from the hotel safe. The desk clerk brought him a large airmail envelope bulging with money. "I wasn't close enough to see if it was lire, francs, or dollars," she said.

Quickly, Vivi left the hotel, carrying away a memory of that parting which has not faded in over three decades: of the tall, elegant man in a double-breasted grey flannel suit, a lonely figure with a gentle smile and haunting eyes.

The next morning Beurling was in Rome where he moved into a hotel near the train station, the Méditerranée. One of Beurling's many assets was his penchant for attracting attention wherever he went; in Rome, the gossip capital of Europe, it was a decided liability in 1948. It was wishful thinking if the Machal had hoped to keep Beurling's presence there a secret.

Within a few hours of settling into the Méditerranée, a functional hostelry situated near the Rome train station, Beurling met another living legend. He was a colourful Swede, the station manager in the Italian capital for the newly organized Scandinavian airlines, SAS. Corpulent and loud the Swede was known to both the Roman and expatriate community as a man whose appetite for good food matched his taste for *la dolce vita*, the good life.

On the evening of May 8, Beurling and the Swede appeared in one of Rome's fashionable bistros, La Biblioteca, a hangout for movie stars, writers, and journalists. On this night a SAS crew was stuck in the Eternal City awaiting repairs to their aircraft.

The crew's captain was a Norwegian who bore a striking resemblance to Beurling. Jack Nyhuus was tall and blond, lean and handsome; like Beurling, Nyhuus was a man of action.*

---

* Nyhuus trained at Toronto Island Airport and later at Little Norway in the Ontario north woods.

Before the war he had been a national skiing champion who was selected to carry the crown jewels of Norway out of the country when war began. Nyhuus had also been a Spitfire pilot in the Royal Norwegian Air Force; he had won his wings in Canada before he was posted to Europe where he had become renowned as a menace to German freight and troop trains. His reputation as a train buster grew as he perfected his strafing technique, a tactic which relied for its success on deflection shooting.

In the midst of the smoky La Biblioteca, Nyhuus and Beurling exchanged stories and details of their respective deflection-shooting techniques. It was a memorable meeting for the Norwegian fighter, an evening of reminiscing, of wine, laughter, and song. At one point the SAS manager, who considered himself something of a Caruso, began to sing an aria. To Nyhuus's surprise Beurling joined in with his baritone voice.

Nyhuus left before the party broke up only to discover the following morning that some of the revellers, including Beurling, had been locked up for the night at a local police station. The owner of the night club had called police when a disturbance broke out. In the end no one was charged with any offence and the police released everyone the morning after. Nevertheless, in a space of a couple of days, all the reporters in town knew that Beurling was in Rome.

No one was more disappointed than Sydney Shulemson back in Montreal when an Israeli called him from New York. "I had gone to so much trouble," he says, "over a period of months to assure the secrecy of his departure for Israel."

Shulemson's major concern was that a "very serious attempt" would be made to assassinate Beurling, and that all of his efforts to shield Beurling from the public eye had been for naught. What Shulemson didn't know was that somewhere between Montreal and Rome, Beurling had telephoned Bruce West, who was now back at *The Globe and Mail* in Toronto.

"I'm off to Israel," Beurling told West on the telephone. "Don't write anything until I get there. I'll send you a postcard." West honoured Beurling's request but it would only be a few days before he was writing the hero's obituary.

After getting out of jail, Beurling became a familiar figure at the Israeli air operation located at Urbe airfield, just north of the city. The Israeli operation was masked by a private flying company called Alica which was operated by a recently retired Italian air-force general, Umberto Kappa, a man of erect bearing and precise manners. Kappa had contracted to train and to give refresher courses to pilots bound for Israel.

One of Kappa's instructors, Captain Massimo Guerrini, was also a veteran pilot of the Italian air force. According to Guerrini the first time the lanky blond Canadian appeared at Alica's hangars, he tried to talk Guerrini's pretty wife into going up for a sightseeing flight over Rome. The retired captain scotched the offer because he said he did not know how good a pilot Beurling was and did not want his wife flying with an unknown pilot.

These were hectic days for Alica. There was an urgency about the operation and a tension that was unbearable, charged by the daily news from Israel.

May 15, 1948, was the first full day of Israeli independence. The new nation awoke to learn that armies from Egypt, Syria, Jordan, Lebanon, and Iraq were on the move. On that day, too, the skies over Israel began to fill with Arab aircraft. By the best count the Arabs had at their command 131 planes, including forty-five fighters and twenty-nine bombers. Among their fighters were late-model Supermarine Spitfires and the perky Italian Macchis. Israel on the other hand counted only twenty-eight airplanes, most of which were light single-engine models hastily converted for wartime. The operative word that went out from Tel Aviv to Europe and across the Atlantic was to get the newly acquired planes to Israel.

All over Europe the frantic airlift went on. Nowhere was the scene more bizarre than at a place called Žatec in Czechoslovakia. Operating from a former Luftwaffe airbase in the once-occupied area of the Sudetenland, Jewish and non-Jewish volunteers were stuffing two DC-4's with arms and ammunition. The Žatec base would prove to be a most vital location from which the badly needed arms, supplies, and aircraft were to pour into Israel.

In the pipeline, too, at Nice were those twenty Canadian-built Norseman freighters, and on Tuesday, May 18, 1948, three of them got flying orders.

One by one the three planes climbed out over the sea. Hugging the coastline, their grey fuselages blending into the silvery sky, they bumped along in the humid air. Soon they passed into Italian air space. Pisa drifted away below them. Corsica lay beyond the starboard wing. Swinging inland over Civitavecchia, just north of Rome, they picked up the Tiber and snaked above it until they reached Forte Antenna, a knob of earth, south of Urbe airfield. Its appearance told the pilots the flight was over. As they taxied to the Alica hangars, the volunteer pilots, who had been sitting around Urbe for two weeks and more, clustered about the planes. On Thursday, it was decided, six pilots would get a shakedown flight in preparation for the longer and more arduous passage to Israel.

On Thursday, Rome awakened to find itself blessed by a warm, windless spring day. It was humid, to be sure, but not intolerably so. The first morning freight and passenger trains had already rattled out of the city, heading north to Italy's big industrial centres. If any rail passengers had glanced to the left as they passed Urbe airfield, they would have seen three grey Canadian bushplanes perched on the grass in front of the corrugated tin hangars of the Alica flying company. A dozen pilots mingled around the aircraft as mechanics topped up the planes' wing tanks. The aircraft bore few markings and they looked somewhat naked sitting there in the morning sun.

George Beurling was one of the pilots picked to check out one of the three aircraft. He was paired with a pilot named Leonard Cohen, an English Jew, who had served in Malta as a RAF pilot during the war. Five years older than the Canadian, Cohen was considered a colourful personality; during the war he had gained the nickname "The King of Lampedusa". The story went that Cohen had affected the surrender of the Island of Lampedusa, off the Italian coast, while experiencing engine failure. Cohen had been forced to land the small flying boat he was piloting in one of the bays of the island. As he ran the aircraft onto the beach, the story goes, he found the Italian garrison drawn up in parade order in front of his airplane, and the officer in charge presented his sword to Cohen in the act of surrender.

On this morning Cohen found himself sitting in a Norseman with Canada's most famous fighter pilot, ready for a routine practice flight. They taxied to the end of the main north–south runway, opened the throttle, and sped across the grass. Shortly they were airborne. It was 11:10 a.m.

Most pilots waiting around airports find it impossible to avert their eyes from an airplane taking off or landing. That's the way it was that morning for Ferrero Giannini. A test pilot during the war, Giannini had become an instructor. That morning he had a lesson scheduled, but the student pilot was late. Standing outside the Alica hangars, Giannini's blue eyes followed the flight of the Norseman which had already made two circuits of the airfield. Now it was banking over Forte Antenna, coming in from the south for a practice landing.

Giannini remembers it was a perfect flying day. Visibility was good. There was only a light wind. He watched the Norseman approach. The plane was 300 feet from the ground, having already completed its approach turn, when Giannini saw a strange flicker along the bottom of the Norseman's fuselage. At first it appeared as a very thin veil of blue vapour. He couldn't make out what it was. As the aircraft floated over the end of the runway, much lower and closer now, Giannini's heart jumped. He saw that it was a sheet of flame, almost imperceptible, but as the Norseman drew closer the flame increased in intensity and stretched the entire length of the aircraft.

"Oh, Mother of God," Giannini said to himself. Others, standing nearby, also watched with disbelief.

The Norseman was now very close to touching the grass runway. As the wheels kissed the ground, suddenly and to the horror of all the bystanders, flames enveloped the fuselage. For the two pilots inside the Norseman, this would have been the first indication that the aircraft had caught fire.

The Norseman was down and the engine raced. Massimo Guerrini was convinced that there had been a last-minute surge of power. Everyone saw the plane turn violently to the left, towards the banks of the Tiber River. Many thought the crew was racing for the water, to plunge the aircraft into the Tiber. It was too late.

There was a thunderous explosion. A huge, orange fireball engulfed the airplane. Mechanics and pilots dashed across the grass, shouting and yelling, but as they neared the burning Norseman, an invisible shield of intense, searing heat stopped them in their tracks. Above the tornado of flame, an ugly black pillar of smoke curled into the blue skies of Rome. Until the fire department arrived, that

pillar of smoke was a cruel memorial to the site of George
Beurling's death, a few feet from the banks of the Tiber
River.

Ironically, too, the crash in Rome was Beurling's tenth.
The Knight of Malta had used up the cat's proverbial nine
lives.

FOURTEEN

The Riddle in Rome

IN MONTREAL, Sydney Shulemson heard the news on his car radio as he drove to work that Thursday morning. Shulemson's first reaction was to assume that Beurling had been murdered.

"I was sick," he remembers. "After all the effort that I had put out, someone, somehow breached my idea of security; that someone had not carried out the instructions that I had insisted upon. It was either that, or Beurling himself had contacted the press. Once he got to Rome, I no longer had control."

When Shulemson arrived at his office there were two telephone messages waiting. One was from an Israeli agent in New York. The second was from Frederick Beurling, George's father. Breaking his own security, Shulemson used his office telephone to call New York to determine whether or not the report was true. Then, with a heavy heart, he got into his car and drove to Grand Boulevard in Notre Dame de Grâce, the west-end district of Montreal where the Beurlings now lived. This was to be his first meeting with Beurling's family.

"They told me that George had told them not to believe any story about his death unless it was confirmed by me personally. I was rather taken aback by this, but I realized that he had concocted all of these ideas and not knowing what I was going to finally decide for him to do, he had told his parents not to belive any story about his death."

Shulemson would have to wait until the following day for the official word. When he got it, he spent the evening consoling Beurling's grieving parents.

The Montreal Star quoted Fred Beurling as saying he had expected his son's life "to end in a blaze of smoke, from the thing he loved the most, an airplane".

In Toronto, Bruce West wrote Beurling's obituary for *The Globe and Mail*. He reminded his readers that there were two George Beurlings—the charming kid with the reckless grin and the cold-blooded fighter pilot, "perhaps the coldest, deadliest human who ever sat behind an aircraft's sights and smiled happily as he watched his foe being blasted to pieces".

Time magazine called him a mercenary "who bargained with both the Arabs and the Jews before accepting the Haganah's offer."

In New York, Ed Sullivan, the *Daily News* columnist, recalled that he had seen Beurling "recently in Manhattan strolling down Fifth Avenue with the beautifully moulded Vivi Stokes (a society girl who doesn't go much for society boys) quite oblivious to the rest of the crowd—an unforgettably handsome pair".

Diana went to work as usual that morning, to her job with the CBC in Montreal. She may have been one of the few people in the city who hadn't heard the news. Around noon when she was leaving her desk to go to lunch it occurred to her fellow workers that Diana hadn't heard of the tragedy. Someone had the courage to tell her.

"It was a bright, clear, sunny day," she remembers. "The sun was really very strong. I went into the restaurant and it was very dark. It occurred to me that this was what life was going to be like without him. He was like the sun and it was like the sun had gone out of all our lives." She cried alone.

In New York around two o'clock in the afternoon, a telephone rang in Vivi Stokes's apartment. There was an overseas call, the operator said. It must be Beurling, she thought, for only the day before she had received a telegram from him urging her to hasten her departure. "Hurry up blue eyes" the message had said. Instead a man's voice she had never heard before was speaking. It was an Israeli officer who was a friend of Beurling. He was sorry to inform her that Beurling had been killed in an airplane accident. "We found your telephone number on a bedside table in his room," the man said, continuing with details of the accident, none of which Vivi remembered; the news left her in a state of shock.

What happened that spring day in Rome? How could one of the most skilled pilots of the Second World War be a victim of such a twist of fate? Was it as simple as a sudden fire on board? Was there any evidence to support Shulemson's suspicion of sabotage and assassination?

Unhappily, there are no satisfactory answers. In the twenty-four hours following the explosion, the wire services in Rome deluged the tickers with stories, night leads, new leads, day leads, sidebars, and official quotes. There was a plethora of information.

The press had reported variously that there had been an explosion in the air. False. The press had reported that there had been an engine failure after take-off. False. The press had reported that Beurling's last act was a most gallant one: that with no engine power, he tried to manoeuvre the crippled aircraft away from a newly built complex of workers' flats. False. There are no highrise buildings near the south end of the Urbe landing field. The press had also reported that Beurling had violated the cardinal rule for a single-engine aircraft if it loses power on take-off: instead of continuing to head into the wind and to put the plane down immediately in a forced landing, reporters said he attempted to return to the field. False.

What did actually happen? The eyewitness accounts of the two experienced Italian pilots standing on the ground, Massimo Guerrini and Ferrero Giannini, given independently, appear to be accurate. Their descriptions of the fatal landing are similar. The Norseman was making a normal approach with appropriate power when the nearly invisible veil of flame appeared below the fuselage at around 300 feet, and by the time the aircraft touched down, it had grown to a sheet of flame running the entire length of the fuselage. Further, when the aircraft turned to the left, the flame engulfed the entire fuselage; the horrendous explosion followed. Their recollections differ in only one aspect. Guerrini heard the engine race after the plane turned; Giannini did not.

More important: why was there a sudden fire explosion? The answer to that question can never be known. There was never an official scientific investigation into Beurling's crash, of the kind the public today has come to expect, involving painstaking reconstruction of wreckage and examination using an electron microscope. The inquiry was conducted by policemen in Rome. There were three reports made to the Ministry of the Interior. The first came only two hours after Beurling and Cohen had been killed. The local carabinieri reported that the Norseman had caught fire "at an elevation of approximately fifty metres, crashing on the ground in flames for causes not yet precise". Eyewitnesses Giannini and Guerrini say the first flame appeared at more than twice that distance from the ground. The plane did not crash but made a normal landing before the explosion occurred.

The initial report, while it identified the crew as Beurling and Cohen, acknowledged that the bodies were burned beyond recognition. One immediately asks how the identification could be made under these circumstances? Was there evidence from others at the field who actually saw Beurling and Cohen climb into the Norseman and take off? There is no explanation.

Later, the same day, a longer accident report was delivered to the Ministry of the Interior. It offered no clearer information. But instead of reporting the height of the Norseman as fifty metres when the flame broke out, it now said the fire appeared when the aircraft was at thirty metres.

Eight days later the final accident-investigation report (which suggested a probable cause) was submitted to the Ministry: "The aeronautical technicians [mechanics] have established that the machine caught fire presumably due to a backfire caused by the engulfment of the carburetor. On account of the little knowledge of this kind of machine it is to be supposed that the pilot would have handled wrongly the controls causing the backfire mentioned previously." As far as the Italian authorities were concerned, the case was closed.

Unfortunately, the three investigation reports were of the most shoddy nature, riddled with errors. Beurling was variously identified as "Beurlinger" and "Beuling". He was identified as being Jewish. The aircraft number was reported as N69822. In subsequent reports the six in the registration number becomes a seven. Can one presume that the error was typographical?

If N69822, a U.S. Federal Aviation Agency registration number, was the correct one, then the Norseman was phony. The FAA records in Oklahoma City show that number had been assigned to only one aircraft, a Timm N2T-1 which was de-registered as of February 4, 1949. Further, the U.S. Air Force Museum at Wright-Patterson Air Force Base in Ohio, confirms that N69822 was not a USAF marking.

Without the Norseman's correct registration number

there could be no complete investigation into the crash: there is absolutely no way to trace the history of the aircraft. And without a history of the aircraft there is no way to find a plausible cause of the crash. The Norseman, for instance, was manufactured in a number of configurations. All were fitted with port and starboard fifty-gallon wing tanks. Other models contained an additional thirty-gallon belly tank, aft of the cockpit. Some were equipped with an electric fuel pump. Was the Norseman in Rome so equipped? The truth is we do not know. Without this most basic and vital information the cause of the crash will remain a mystery and the carabinieri's suggestion of a "backfire" can only be speculation.

What of the possibility of sabotage? Given the emotionally charged atmosphere of the times, it was not unnatural for Jews to seize on such a suspicion. On the day of the crash, bitter fighting was raging in Jerusalem. The Arab Legion was ravaging the Jewish quarter in the Old City. The possibility that hundreds of Jews would be liquidated in the fierce shelling and fighting was grimly real. The strange circumstances in Rome were seen by Jews as the work of assassins.

There was little security at Urbe airport in those days. The Italian pilots who congregated there, most of them ex-air-force fliers, were an informal bunch. They were enjoying the forgotten casual ways of civilians. A few feet from where the Alica operation was based, a main road passes the airfield. The Norseman airplanes had sat unguarded for two days before Beurling's flight. It would have been relatively easy for a saboteur to tamper with any aircraft on the tarmac. Did someone tinker with the gas lines or the fuel selectors?

The Israelis themselves made an attempt to find out what happened at Urbe; but since there was no organization at the time capable of conducting an investigation several thousand miles away on another country's sovereign soil, their findings too were inconclusive.

The suggestion by the carabinieri that the pilot "handled wrongly the controls" must also be studied. Beurling had amassed over 4,000 flying hours, many of these under the most trying combat conditions; yet, following the war, his flying time was quite limited. Despite today's glossy magazine ads trumpeting the glories of flight and the ease with which they suggest anyone can learn to fly, flying is a serious undertaking. Being a professional pilot is demanding; it is a discipline that requires enormous concentration, good health, and a perfect mental attitude. Even the most experienced pilots with many thousands of flying hours who do not fly within specified intervals are required by law to be checked out by qualified instructors, in some cases by instructors whose flying hours don't match those of the man being re-examined. From the records we know that Beurling's licence had lapsed. Was he getting rusty? What was his physical condition? Was he fit?

Had Beurling flown a Norseman previously? In one interview he claimed to a reporter he had been hired to fly a charter trip in a Norseman to Canada's Gaspé region.

Since there was never an official inquest or autopsy, we have, to this day, no official cause of death. Were the two victims conscious or not? How did they die? By suffocation? Or did the explosion kill them? The deaths are shrouded in mystery. And because the bodies were so horribly disfigured in the searing heat of a fire so intense that it liquified some metal parts of the aircraft, there is no certainty as to which of the two was on the left-hand side where the captain of the flight is seated. Who was the pilot? The investigation reports neglected to tell us.

How could the Canadian government allow the events of May 20, 1948, and all the doubts created by an inadequate investigation, to go unexamined?

It is fair to say that the Italian government was most anxious to end the affair; its tepid police inquiry certainly shows a bureaucratic haste to settle the matter as quickly and as quietly as possible. The investigation lasted exactly eight days. Politically it was an extremely sensitive situation, since many Italians were sympathetic to the Jewish cause. To launch an exhaustive investigation was simply an embarrassment. It would have exposed the fact that Italy was turning a blind eye to the shipment of arms and men to Israel from Italian soil, a disclosure that would put both Britain and the United States in a difficult position. If the extent of the operations were detailed, the two world powers, the former involved in a naval blockade of Palestine, and the latter in an arms embargo, would have to react. Although both world powers knew privately what was happening, officially it was best left in the shadows of doubt and speculation.

But how could Canada react so coldly to the news that its greatest warrior was dead? With Canada's close ties to Britain, and given the British position towards Palestine, Beurling's involvement was most embarrassing. But more important perhaps was a decided lack of public opinion regarding his death. Canadians were so weary of the old war, which was taking an insufferably long time to pass (energy and food controls were still in effect in 1948) that they had little interest in a new war half a world away. Besides, the *Maclean's* and *New Liberty* articles in which Beurling was portrayed as a dedicated mercenary were there for all to read. The *Maclean's* article appeared on the newsstands a few days before the fatal crash, providing Canadians with an up-to-the-minute account of the ace's life at the very moment the Italians were preparing to bury him.

While the Italians were remiss in their investigation,

they made up for the shortcoming with the grandest of funerals.

Following the crash, Beurling's body was taken to the morgue of Santo Spirito Hospital within the shadow of the Vatican. On Saturday, May 22, the body was placed in a plain, closed pine coffin, and carried to a vaulted obituary chamber in the hospital where the Italian press said it would "lie in state" until the funeral. Hundreds of Italian Jews came to mourn the Knight of Malta who died so tragically.

On Monday, an ornate hearse, drawn by two black horses, wound its melancholy path from Santo Spirito, through the palm-lined Piazza Cavour to the doors of Rome's Waldensian Church. Hundreds, perhaps as many as a thousand mourners, walked in silence behind the hearse. It was a strange cortège.

The Canadian embassy sent its delegates. High-ranking officers of the Italian air force, bemedalled and plumed, saluted the body of their former enemy. The Chief Rabbi of Rome led a procession of Jews. All over Rome that day, Jewish shopkeepers had clanged down the shutters of their stores as a salute to the young Canadian who died on the road to Jerusalem.

Inside the spacious Protestant church, a guard of six Polish boy scouts flanked the coffin. At the foot of the bier someone had placed a wreath on whose ribbon were the words "Royal Air Force".

The service, conducted by the pastor of Rome's Waldensian congregation, was simple and short, and the Chief Rabbi delivered the eulogy in Italian and Hebrew.

The funeral lacked only one element. Beurling's widow, family, and personal friends were not in attendance. In New York Vivi Stokes was beside herself with grief, torn by her decision not to attend, believing that her appearance would needlessly disturb the family. It was a decision that she has since regretted, for if she had gone, Vivi would have been Beurling's only friend at the funeral.

Shortly after six o'clock in the evening the hearse set off from the church. For a short distance the route to the cemetery followed the banks of the Tiber. It was a warm and balmy evening and all along the way as the horses moved by, the patrons of the open cafes rose in silence — including an old war veteran who saluted the passing cortège. The procession ended at Verano Cemetery, Rome's burial place for Catholics. There the casket was carried from the hearse and placed before a vault.

Those close to the simple wooden coffin noticed a small brass plate on its lid. One word in the inscription seemed oddly out of place. Some unknown Italian had conferred upon the young Canadian in death a rank that he could never have achieved in life. Did he assume that someone so young and brave could not die as a mere flight lieutenant or captain? Those who pressed close to read the words gleaming there in the sun, saw this inscription:

Colonel Georgio Beurling
26 Years of Age
Died 20.5.1948

The Italians had honoured him with the rank equivalent to Group Captain, a lofty air-force grade which the RCAF would have never bestowed and one that Beurling would have detested, since in his opinion anyone over the rank of wing commander was a "son of a bitch".

FIFTEEN

A Short, Troubled Life

ROME, 1948. The end of the summer. The lovely American blonde sitting alone on the sunny terrace did not go unnoticed. A young couple, who stood at the entrance of the outdoor café of the Quirinale Hotel recognized her immediately, and wound their way to her table. The man was an Israeli officer, the woman his wife. Vivi Stokes watched them approach the table, thinking how solemn the man looked for someone so young. Seated now, both the man and his wife offered condolences, their phrases punctuated by the snapping exhaust of motorscooters in the street beyond. Perhaps, the man said, as he produced a manila envelope, Vivi would like to keep the colonel's effects. Vivi took the package, on which was written the name "Colonel Buerling". It annoyed her that the name was misspelled. Struggling to remain composed, Vivi opened the envelope and emptied the contents on the white tablecloth. There was a watch, a pen, a pocketknife, and the little fur monkey, still attached to its elastic string. Gently she took the monkey, put it in her purse, and returned the other articles to the envelope. She thanked the man and the woman, excused herself, and left the restaurant.

It had been a terrible summer for Vivi Stokes, a summer of grief that had kept her in deep melancholy since that awful day in May. Worse was the thought that no one

Beurling had known well had come to the funeral. Nothing, however, had prepared her for the visit to Verano Cemetery. The casket in fact had not been buried. It was instead being stored in a musty warehouse which to Vivi looked more like the freight room at the Rome train station. "I was shocked by the ugliness of it all," she recalled years later, "so thoroughly unsuitable for a man of his stature."

Vivi angrily demanded an explanation. An official told her that no one had claimed the body. Also, because ninety days had passed since his death, burial was now left to the discretion of the authorities. Vivi accepted the responsibility for burial.

The next day she went immediately to Rome's Protestant cemetery and asked to see the director, a "dapper little Italian shaped like a penguin," Vivi says, "a man with a heart of gold" named Marcello Piermattei. Together they strolled through the well-cared-for grounds in search of a suitable resting place.

Vivi found a plot midway between those of the two poets, John Keats and Percy Bysshe Shelley, whose simple graves have drawn admirers to Rome for decades. When Vivi indicated that it was perfectly located, Piermattei sighed, and said, "Madame, this is reserved." When she inquired by whom, he answered, "By me."

Nevertheless, she found a suitable plot nearby and preparations began. The coffin was brought from storage at Verano and the digging of a fresh grave was begun under the supervision of Piermattei.

"I sat quietly for hours on a bench in a dark crypt while the grave was being prepared," Vivi recalls. "I cannot remember the presence of anyone except Mr. Piermattei. As desperate as I was, it seemed nevertheless such a small tribute to pay a remarkable man who had brought such happiness into my life. Mr. Piermattei had complete understanding of my unusual situation and no embarrassing questions were asked, only those required for legal reasons."

Earlier Vivi had ordered a plain silver cross to be fixed to the coffin, which bore Beurling's name, rank, and the date of his death.

On the back of the cross Vivi directed that the following line from a Shakespeare sonnet be engraved: "And Thou . . . hast all/The all of me."

So on Vivi's orders the body of the fallen hero was laid to rest in a grave near Keats and Shelley, a shaded spot, to sleep the sleep of poets under the cypress trees of Rome.

"At twilight the cemetery closed its gates and Mr. Piermattei drove me back to Parioli [a district of Rome] where I was staying. It was only then in his car that I broke down. Before, I had been too shocked and numbed by what had, and had not, happened. I longed for a hand to hold or a shoulder to lean on, but I was completely and utterly alone."

Word of Vivi's action reached Beurling's parents in Montreal. Greatly agitated, they contacted Sydney Shulemson.

"I distinctly recall how upset the family was," Shulemson remembers. "I told them, 'if the body had to be moved, we'll move it. We don't want you to be unhappy.' They asked if it would be possible to bury him in Israel. And that's what I arranged." For the Beurling family, believers in the tenets of the Plymouth Brethren, the austere sect that rejected all the trappings of ritualistic worship, the thought that their son was buried in Rome, with all its papal pageantry, was anathema.

Diana, who was legally Beurling's widow, consented. She gave her permission for the remains to be disinterred and removed to Israel.

On the morning of November 9, 1950, two and one-half years after the fatal crash, two caskets, one bearing the body of George Beurling, the other holding the remains of Leonard Cohen, arrived in a military aircraft at the airport of Israel's northern port city of Haifa.

The coffins, draped with the blue and white Israeli flag, were laid in state at a nearby air-force base, where an honour guard of young airmen mounted a silent watch. In the early afternoon there was a long funeral procession through the streets of Haifa. Israeli air-force planes, flying low over the city, saluted the men who had died in Rome on their way to Israel.

Once again, hundreds gathered at the services which were conducted by an Anglican minister.

The military cemetery is located at the foot of Mount Carmel, near the cave of the Prophet Elijah, the messenger of the Messiah. There, the boy from Verdun, Canada's great war hero, finally found in death the peace that had eluded him in life.

The grave is marked, as are the others in the Zahal Cemetery, with only name, rank, and serial number. The practical Israelis correctly buried him as a *segen*, a captain, the equivalent rank of flight lieutenant.

* * *

George Beurling's life was short and turbulent. A paradoxical, solitary man, he sought and created a public image with the help of his numerous contacts in the press. He was disorderly and disrespectful, yet a supremely talented pilot and gunner. He was warm and sentimental—a romantic, if there ever was one—yet capable of being cruel, callous, and mercenary. In the end, after he had successfully hidden his basic humanity from the public, the publicity he adored dried up; the public rejected a hero who was flawed.

He was after all a self-educated boy from a working-class family who suddenly, almost overnight, became a celebrity, a front-page figure, a hero. His insecurity and resentment at being forced to accept a commission caused his rebellious nature to flare up. He got back at "them" in a most petulant and childish way — a disregard for the codes of dress and a lack of respect for higher ranks.

Did Beurling have reason for his hostility to the RCAF? Without doubt. They had rejected him. Were their reasons justified? Probably so, given the state of the air force when war broke out, an air force without airplanes or a plan to meet the emergency.*

More important and more simply put, Beurling was a misfit, a great pilot indeed but a poor soldier. Military life is extremely rigid, marked by tradition and discipline. Moreover, in the military, as elsewhere, there are two types of orders — the orders you give, and the orders you take. George Beurling never fitted into this strictly disciplined, tightly arranged system. He found it difficult to give orders and even more difficult to take them.

Throughout his military career Beurling alienated himself from authority. It is reasonable to assume that his various detractors, if asked, could hardly offer enthusiastic recommendations on behalf of the former flying ace.

Airline executives making informal enquiries of a well-placed air marshal concerning a character reference — an informal one, you understand — about this chap Beurling, might be forgiven for hiring less flamboyant pilots. Those minor altercations came back to haunt Beurling after the war. Why else would this gifted pilot have had such difficulty finding work?

And what about the press? Beurling's good relations

---

* It is unfair to lay blame on the existing officer corps in the RCAF in 1939. They were dedicated men, but for years were denied the money required to develop an effective air arm to fight a war that most people knew was inevitable.

with editors and newsmen were obvious. He sought publicity unashamedly and, in return for his stories, reporters
pampered him.

Did Beurling make a conscious ideological commitment to fight with the Jews, as Sydney Shulemson and
Ben Dunkelman insist? It certainly makes sense that
George Beurling, with his strict religious upbringing,
would have been acutely aware of the light the Old Testament cast on the 1948 Arab—Israeli War. And yet, why did
he claim to Vivi Stokes (the person he was closest to) that
he had taken the job in order to get rich quick? Why did he
tell newsmen and other fliers the same thing? Was he in
fact a mercenary? The men who engaged him steadfastly
maintain that money was neither offered nor paid. Further, no compensation was ever paid by the Israeli government to his widow or his family.

What about the bizarre suggestion from Vivi Stokes
that he may have been a double agent, perhaps a triple
agent? Was that a possibility, one that accounted for his
apparent affluence in her presence? Yet his widow's recollections during those final months in Montreal of a man
stalking the streets waiting to borrow money from her are
sad and ignominious, but more important, contradictory.
Had Beurling planned it as part of an elaborate cover-up?
Some clues might have been found in the horrible crash in
Rome but the cause of the accident remains a mystery
more than three decades later. Like so many other questions about Beurling's life, these too are unanswerable.

In 1948, time was passing George Beurling by. He had
already become an anachronistic figure in a world that
would soon face new kinds of warfare, the politics of the
Cold War heralded by the Berlin airlift, and only two
years after his death, one that would witness, in Korea, the
first jet war.

A few weeks after Beurling's burial, Vivi Stokes, back

in her New York apartment, turned to the writings of Antoine de Saint-Exupéry. This French writer was himself fascinated by the freedom of flight and the dark, unfathomable power of war. Sometime that spring, Beurling too had read the same words, a short passage which he had underlined. It read: "I hate this century with all of my heart. A man can die of thirst in it."

* * *

Not long ago, in February 1979, the former Spitfire pilot, and later portrait painter, Robert Hyndman, sat in his studio in the Gatineau Hills, north of Ottawa. He had been talking about Beurling. The conversation had ended and the artist mused over the cold landscape outside with its clumps of black alder rattling in the wind. The fading light had turned the snow as blue as steel.

"Christ," Hyndman suddenly burst out, "what a waste!"

He hadn't thought of George Beurling for many years. Now when he did, the recollection made him grieve.

* * *

It was early in the evening February 26, 1960, when an Alitalia DC-7 taxied along the tarmac at Shannon Airport in Ireland waiting for permission to take off.

"Cleared for take-off, zero-five," a controller's voice suddenly crackled in the airliner cockpit.

"Zero-five," the captain acknowledged. "Thank you, Shannon tower."

A few seconds later the aircraft was airborne, turning to the left as it climbed into the sky. Eyewitnesses were startled when the airliner continued to turn instead of climbing. Seconds later it exploded on the ground, killing thirty-four of the fifty-two on board.

Two months later a package arrived at the apartment of

Vivi Stokes in New York. A letter from the airlines regretted the damage to some personal effects which she had shipped by air freight on the fatal flight. When she examined the contents Vivi found stuck at the bottom of the package the little monkey that George Beurling had won at a Broadway shooting gallery twelve years before. As she picked up the prize she shook with horror and revulsion for she could see that the monkey had been terribly charred by the flames of the crash.

Epilogue

LADDIE LUCAS now lives in a fashionable flat in London. He left the RAF after the war and distinguished himself in a variety of careers. He sat in the House of Commons, led the British Walker Cup team, became chairman of the Greyhound Racing Association, and took up writing.

Stan Grant, Beurling's first squadron commander in Malta, stayed in the RAF. Grant rose to the rank of Air Vice-Marshal before he retired. He now lives in a small town in France.

Ferrero Giannini, who witnessed the crash in Rome, is retired at age seventy. He can still be found at Urbe airport watching planes land and take off.

Few of the pilots who flew with Beurling continued to fly once the war was over. One who did was Andy MacKenzie, who survived two years as a prisoner of war in Korea. Today he lives in the Ottawa area where he breeds Newfoundland and Akita dogs.

Jack Nyhuus enjoyed a remarkable postwar career in civil aviation. After rising to senior pilot with SAS he emigrated to Canada in the early 1950s and served with distinction the Department of Transport. Later he became an adviser to Third World countries on aviation planning for the United Nations. Recently, returning to his post in Thailand, he was honoured by the invitation of a trans-

Pacific carrier to take the controls of a 747 Jumbo in the left-hand seat as the behemoth of modern-day aviation floated towards Asia through the velvet, tropical night.

H. H. C. Holderness, who survived the air crash in Scotland with Beurling, returned to Rhodesia where he became a barrister and solicitor. Upon retirement he took up residence in France.

Johnnie Johnson is also retired. He too made the air force a career, leaving it as an Air Vice-Marshal with an impressive collection of honours (the CB, CBE, DSO, DFC, and DL).

The Cochand brothers left the Laurentians long ago. Louis lives in Florida, and Emile, Jr., in Hawaii. Both are involved in the travel business.

Sydney Shulemson remained in Montreal. Every week he rides CN's Via Rail Express to Toronto on business. He won't fly anymore.

Ben Dunkelman is still a dedicated Zionist, dividing his time between art and sailing. He is also the national commander of the Jewish War Veterans of Canada.

With the exception of George's mother who died on April 4, 1974, all members of the Beurling family have survived him. They now live in Ontario.

Diana has re-married, has two children and lives on the west coast.

Vivi Stokes, who became Contessa Crespi, lives in the eastern United States and elsewhere.

The locations which figured so prominently in Beurling's life have, with few exceptions, changed little. The Alica hangar is still standing at Urbe airfield and is now used by the Aero Club di Roma. The take-off run is now paved.

So is the airstrip at Takali in Malta, now a strangely quiet place on weekdays. On weekends, though, it is quite noisy. Local Maltese youths use it for drag races.

The Xara Palace Hotel in Mdina, and its terrace, still offers the most spectacular view of Malta. One hopes Mr. Lucas will consent to visit his old battleground. The food has improved greatly.

Except for Beurling's medals, which are held by the family, few personal artifacts remain. The Tiger Moth has vanished. The Department of Transport tried to find it in the summer of 1950 to cancel its certificates of registration and air-worthiness, but to no avail. It was last seen about that time sitting in a field in Terrebonne, Quebec. (For former pilots, who trained in the British Commonwealth Air Training Plan, BSX carried the RCAF marking 2363.)

Hugh Godefroy left the air force, studied medicine, and now practises in the southern United States.

Faliero Gelli (perhaps the only man ever to survive an attack by Beurling) was repatriated to Italy as a POW where he continued to live until recently, when he emigrated to the United States.

The official oil portrait of George Beurling, painted by Edwin Headly Holgate, is not available for public viewing. It is kept in storage by the Canadian War Museum. There are photographs, of course, but exactly how many is not known. They are among millions of pictures in the Public Archives of Canada which have not been catalogued because of lack of funds.

In Verdun the only reminder of the famous son is the boulevard which carries Beurling's name.

Appendix

THE TERM "ace" is an unofficial one. It seems to have its origin in the French excadrilles of the First World War, when anyone who scored ten or more aerial victories earned the honour. After the Americans arrived in France they arbitrarily set the figure at five. There it remains.

Originally, in order to be credited with an official kill, a pilot required an eyewitness. Later, pictures from gun cameras were accepted as sufficient evidence. In the case of night dogfights, a pilot was awarded a victory if a radar operator confirmed that the enemy blip vanished from the screen.

Attempting to list victories accurately has become a tedious and frustrating undertaking for aviation writers, since different air forces use different methods in recording the kills. For instance, it is the practice in some American units to count as kills aircraft that are destroyed on the ground.

The list that follows shows the top ten Canadian aces in the RAF and the RCAF. The list does not include aircraft destroyed on the ground.

There is some confusion regarding Beurling's score. Official records themselves are contradictory, crediting him with a final total of both $31\frac{1}{3}$ and $29\frac{1}{3}$. Some controversy revolves around two of Beurling's "probably destroyed" enemy aircraft. For this examination the total

183

figure of 31⅓ is given. The one-third figure was credited to Beurling when he and two other pilots attacked an enemy airplane at the same time and it could not be determined who actually shot it down. So all three got part credit. The other Canadian pilots are also given credit for "probably destroyed" aircraft in the figures which appear below.

The second summary lists the Canadian, British, American, and European fliers who became the top Allied aces in the Second World War. In one or two cases the order of their appearance may differ from some previously published lists, most notably the decision to put Squadron Leader St. John Pattle at the head; but to the best of my knowledge, the choice is a fair one.

A word, too, about the German aces. Many of them are credited with victories in the hundreds. Although the claims raise obvious questions, most aviation historians are inclined to accept them. The American aviation writer, Edward H. Sims, for example, explains the number in several ways. The highest-scoring German aces, without exception, served on the Eastern Front. For the most part, German fighter pilots were not restricted to combat tours; they simply flew until they got killed or captured. The highest-scoring fighter pilot in history was Erich Hartmann, a German. He is credited with an incredible 352 victories. Even more remarkable is the fact that he survived the war, as well as ten years in a Russian prison. He was released in 1955.

Finally, the world of the fighter pilot was not exclusively a male one. Women flew in single-combat roles in the Soviet Union. The country's top woman ace was Lieutenant Lilya Litvak, with twelve victories. She was killed in action.

THE LEADING CANADIAN ACES OF THE SECOND WORLD WAR

	Rank	Name	Victories	Awards	Home Town
1.	Flight Lieutenant	George F. Beurling*	31⅓	DSO, DFC, DFM and Bar	Verdun, Que.
2.	Squadron Leader	Vernon C. Woodward	25	DFC and Bar	Victoria, B.C.
3.	Wing Commander	Edward F. J. Charles	22	DSO, DFC and Bar	Lashburn, Sask.
4.	Squadron Leader	Henry W. McLeod**	20	DSO, DFC and Bar	Regina, Sask.
5.	Wing Commander	James F. Edwards	16½	DFC and Bar, DFM	Nokomis, Sask.
6.	Squadron Leader	William T. Klersy*	16½	DSO, DFC and Bar	Brantford, Ont.
7.	Flying Officer	William L. McKnight**	16½	DFC and Bar	Edmonton, Alta.
8.	Squadron Leader	John F. McElroy	16	DFC and Bar	Kamloops, B.C.
9.	Wing Commander	Robert W. McNair***	16	DFC and Two Bars	Battleford, Sask.
10.	Group Captain	P. S. Turner	16	DSO, DFC and Bar	Toronto, Ont.

*   Killed in a flying accident
**   Killed in action
*** Deceased

THE LEADING ALLIED ACES OF THE SECOND WORLD WAR

	Rank	Name	Victories	Nationality	Air Force
1.	Squadron Leader	Marmaduke E. St. John Pattle**	41	South African	RAF
2.	Major	Richard I. Bong***	40	American	USAAF
3.	Group Captain	James E. Johnson	38	British	RAF
4.	Major	Thomas B. McGuire***	38	American	USAAF
5.	Group Captain	C. A. G. Malan***	35	South African	RAF
6.	Captain	David McCampbell	34	American	U.S. Navy
7.	Squadron Leader	Pierre Clostermann	33	French	RAF
8.	Wing Commander	Brendan E. Finucane**	32	Irish	RAF
9.	Flight Lieutenant	George F. Beurling*	31⅓	Canadian	RAF-RCAF
10.	Wing Commander	John Braham	29	British	RAF
	Wing Commander	Robert Tuck	29	British	RAF

    * Killed in a flying accident
   ** Killed in action
 *** Deceased

Acknowledgments

A GREAT NUMBER OF PEOPLE helped during the research on *Hero*, but three especially deserve my sincerest gratitude, no one more than Contessa Vivi Crespi whose patience and understanding was nothing less than epic. Without her help this story could not have been completed. I'm especially grateful to two close friends — Patrick Watson, for asking wise questions and for offering his encouragement and my neighbour, Tony Stachiw, who not only displayed a remarkable knowledge of aviation history, but a dedication to getting the facts right.

I thank, too, Diana Whittall Gardner, George Beurling's widow, for her candour. P. B. "Laddie" Lucas, DSO, DFC, and Peter Jennings in London were most helpful. So was another old friend in Rome, Robert O. Miller. I must thank, too, Sydney S. Shulemson, DSO, DFC, for breaking a thirty-year silence to tell the story behind Beurling's decision to join the Machal in the first Arab–Israeli War of 1948. I am grateful for the help of Michael Rose in my researches in Quebec, and to Judith Poitras in Vancouver.

In Ottawa I'm indebted to Dr. W. A. B. Douglas, Director, Directorate of History, National Defence Headquarters, and to Dr. James Downey, former Vice-President of Carleton University, and Dr. G. Stuart Adam, Director, of the School of Journalism, who supported and encouraged my research.

Since Ottawa was my base of operations, many energetic public servants in various government departments provided me with invaluable assistance. I thank Senator George C. Van Roggen; Admiral Robert Falls, former Chief of the Defence Staff; Peter Magwood, Veterans' Affairs; Jacques Gagné and George Bova, Public Archives. Mrs. William Kincaid, MBE, at the British High Commission, who has always been so helpful in previous projects, was no less so in this undertaking.

In Malta, Philip Vella and John Agius, of the National War Museum Association, were most kind to me when I visited their sunny republic, and undertook to provide me with additional research material after I had left.

I am also grateful to Nicholas Cox, head of research, Public Record Office in Richmond, Surrey, and his associates C. A. Blakeburn, and F. F. Lambert.

In Italy, Nicola Malizia will never know how important his contribution was in breaking the log jam of official bureaucracy.

In Ottawa, the former Italian Ambassador to Canada, His Excellency Georgio Smoquina, also went out of his way to assist me.

Two friends—Calvin Fentress, in New York, and Bruce Innes, in Los Angeles—were most patient in checking out leads and supplying me with new information, as was Melba G. Burns, of the Department of Transportation, Federal Aviation Administration, in Oklahoma City.

The respective staffs at Buckingham Palace and the Imperial War Museum were very thoughtful, too.

An old newspaper friend at the Hamilton *Spectator*, Bob Hanley, also provided me with a lead that eventually opened many doors.

To the staff of the Secretariat at the School of Journalism, Carleton University, I extend my gratitude, espe-

Professors Alan Frizzell, Patrick MacFadden, and Jay Weston could always be counted on to provide good counsel along the way. My thanks, too, for the help I received from two undergraduates in the School of Journalism, Mark Jodoin and Wendy Rajala.

Selected Bibliography

BOOKS

Austin, Dennis. *Malta and the End of Empire*. London: Frank Cass & Co., 1971.

Beurling, George F., and Roberts, Leslie. *Malta Spitfire: The Story of A Fighter Pilot*. Toronto: Oxford University Press, 1943.

Boissevan, Jeremy. *Hal-Farrug: A Village in Malta*. New York: Holt, Rinehart and Winston, 1965.

Chalfont, Alun. *Montgomery of Alamein*. London: Weidenfeld and Nicholson, 1976.

Collins, Larry, and Lapierre, Dominique. *O Jerusalem!* New York: Simon and Schuster, 1972.

Cosgrove, Edmund. *Canada's Fighting Pilots*. Toronto: Clarke, Irwin, 1965.

Deighton, Len. *Fighter: The True Story of the Battle of Britain*. London: Jonathan Cape, 1977.

Deziel, Julien J. *History of Verdun, 1676-1976*. Ottawa: Centennial Committee, 1976.

Dunkelman, Ben. *Dual Allegiance*. Toronto: Macmillan of Canada, 1976.

Ellis, Frank H. *Canada's Flying Heritage*. Toronto: University of Toronto Press, 1954.

England, Robert. *Twenty Million World War Veterans*. Toronto: Oxford University Press, 1950.

Gann, Ernest K. *Ernest K. Gann's Flying Circus*. New York: Macmillan Publishing Co., 1974.

Halliday, Hugh. *The Tumbling Sky*. Stittsville: Canada's Wing, 1978.

Hess, W. N. *The Allied Aces of World War II*. Famous Airmen Series. New York: A. G. Leonard Morgan, 1966.

Irving, David. *The Trail of the Fox*. New York: E. P. Dutton, 1977.

Johnson, J. E. "Johnnie". *Wing Leader*. Toronto: Clarke, Irwin, 1956.

Laspina, S., The Very Rev. Mgr. *Outlines of Maltese History*. Malta: A.C. Aquilina, 1966.

Lucas, "Laddie". *Five Up: A Chronicle of Five Lives*. London: Sidgwick & Jackson, 1978.

Manchester, William. *The Glory and the Dream*. Boston and Toronto: Little, Brown and Company, 1974.

Molson, K. M. *Pioneering in Canadian Air Transport*. Winnipeg: James Richardson & Sons, 1974.

Niven, David. *The Moon's A Balloon*. New York: G. P. Putnam's Sons, 1972.

O'Callaghan, Kevin. *Malta: A Handbook to the Republic*. London: Palmerstone Press, 1964.

Parrish, Thomas, ed. *The Simon and Schuster Encyclopedia of World War II*. New York: Simon and Schuster, 1978.

Poolman, Kenneth. *Faith, Hope and Charity*. London: William Kimber & Co., 1954.

Price, Alfred. *Spitfire — A Documented History*. London: Macdonald and Jane's, 1977.

Ramsey, Winston G., ed. *After the Battle, Number 10: Malta During WW II*. London: Battle of Britain Prints International, 1975.

Revie, Alistair; Foster, Thomas; and Graham, Burton. *Battle: A History of Conflict on Land, Sea and Air*. London: Marshall Cavendish, 1977.

Richards, Denis. *The Royal Air Force, 1939-1945*. Vol. 1. London: H.M.S.O., 1953.

Rubenstein, Murray, and Goldman, Richard. *Shield of David: An Illustrated History of the Israeli Air Force*. Englewood Cliffs, N.J.: Prentice-Hall, 1978.

Shirer, William L. *Berlin Diary*. New York: Alfred A. Knopf, 1940.

Sims, Edward, H. *The Greatest Aces*. New York: Harper & Row, 1967.

Tallman, Frank. *Flying the Old Planes*. New York: Doubleday & Company, 1973.

Toland, John. *Adolf Hitler*. New York: Doubleday & Company, 1976.

Waugh, Evelyn. *When the Going Was Good*. London: Duckworth, 1946.

Winton, John. *Air Power at Sea, 1939-45*. London: Griffin House, 1976.

Woods, Walter S. *Rehabilitation — A Combined Operation*. Ottawa: Queen's Printer, 1953.

PERIODICALS AND NEWSPAPERS

Airforce Magazine, Ottawa
The Daily Express, London
The Daily News, New York
The Globe and Mail, Toronto
The Gazette, Montreal
Maclean's, Toronto
Malta This Month, Valletta
The Manchester Guardian

Messaggero, Rome
Momento Sera, Rome
The Montreal Daily Star
The Montreal Standard
New Liberty
The New York Journal American
The New York Times
Nuovo Giornale D'Italia, Rome
The Ottawa Journal
Reader's Digest
The Times, London
The Times, Malta

WIRE SERVICES

Associated Press
British United Press
Canadian Press

AUDIO AND VISUAL

The British Broadcasting Corporation
The Canadian Broadcasting Corporation
Fox Movietone News
Public Archives of Canada, Sound and Film Departments

Index

"Aces":
derivation of term, 183
German, 184
Soviet, 187
top ten Allied, 186
top ten Canadian, 185
Afrika Korps. *See* Rommel,
Erwin
Alborán Basin, 41
Aldrich, Wilfrid, 93-94
Alica, 156, 157, 158, 166, 180
Arab–Israeli War (1948), 137-76
Army Air Corps, 114
Aviation in Canada:
1920s, 13-15
1940s, 14*n*
Aviron Company, 150

Battle of Britain, 27, 30, 74
Beechcraft, 112
Berlin Diary (Shirer), 35
Beurling, David, 8, 59*n*, 79, 85,
133, 180
Beurling, Elsie, 8, 180
Beurling, Frederick, 7-8, 12,
16-18, 23, 79, 161, 162, 180
Beurling, George "Buzz":
early life, 7-20
early interest in aviation, 7-8,
15-16, 17-18

religious upbringing, 8-10, 12,
29-30, 116, 142
facility with languages, 11, 152
first flight, 15-16
first solo flight, 16
education, 16-17
skills in mathematics, 17,
54-56
turned down by RCAF, 21-23
enlists with RAF, 21-23
near-fatal crashes, 26, 31-32,
70, 73, 77-78, 93, 94, 100-01
with Initial Training Wing
(RAF), 24-25
in No. 5 Elementary Training
School (RAF), 24-25
in No. 8 Service Flying
School (RAF), 25-28
in Operational Training Unit
No. 57 (RAF), 29
in Volunteer Reserve (RAF),
24-33
in 403 Squadron (RAF), 30-31
in 41 Squadron (RAF), 31-33,
48
in Gibraltar, 41-43
on H.M.S. *Eagle*, 41-44
in Malta, 1-5, 45-75
in 249 Squadron (RAF), 1-5,
47-64

remarkable eyesight, 49,
52–53
skill at deflection shooting,
53–56
nicknamed "Screwball", 59,
59n
awarded Distinguished
Flying Medal and Bar, 61
shoots down Faliero Gelli,
64–66
strain of combat on, 66–68, 85
accepts officer's commission,
67
airmanship, 69–70
awarded Distinguished
Flying Cross, 74
awarded Distinguished
Service Order, 74
ordered home from Malta,
74–75
reunited with his family, 79
meets with Prime Minister
Mackenzie King, 79–81
honoured at reception at
Verdun Auditorium, 81–84
involvement with Victory
Loan Drive, 74, 83
recounting of July 12, 1942,
hit, 84–85
statement made in first press
interview in Canada, 85
and Diana Gardner, 87–88,
115–25, 134, 135–36, 148
transfers from RAF to RCAF,
88–89
at Royal Investiture, 92
posted to Central Gunnery
School, 92–96
swearing into RCAF, 95–96
posted to 403 Squadron
(RCAF), 96–106

promoted to flight lieutenant,
103–04
grounded, 105–06
transferred to 412 Squadron
(RCAF), 106–10
last victory in combat, 108
repatriated to Canada, 109–10
arrives in Halifax, 111
with No. 3 Training
Command (RCAF), 112
resigns from RCAF, 112–14
turned down by Army Air

Beurling, Gladys, 8, 79, 180
Beurling, Hetty Florence, 7, 8,
79, 180
Beurling, Richard, 8, 79, 180
La Biblioteca (Rome), 154–55
Bowater, Lady, 117
Breadner, Air Marshal L. S., 109
Brethren's Bible Hall
(Montreal), 9
British Commonwealth Air
Training Plan, 151, 181
British Eighth Army, 38
Brooke, Rupert, 126
Buchanan, W. J. "Bucky", 14
Buckham, Robert, 93, 103

Campbell, Air Vice-Marshal
H. L., 129
Canadian Jewish Congress, 139
"Canadian Tiger", 141, 144, 148
Cape Breton Flying Club,
132–33
Cartierville (Quebec), 15–16
Central Gunnery School, 92–96
Chalet Cochand, 119–21
Chez George (New York), 152
Chicken Coop (Montreal), 115,
136, 148

Chinese National Air Force, 130
Churchill, Winston, 39
Civitavecchia (Italy), 157
Clare, John, 134, 146-47
Clough-Ormiston, Kathleen
    Marie, 106-07
Coach and Horses (London), 94
Cochand, Emile, Jr., 119, 121,
    180
Cochand, Emile, Sr., 119
Cochand, Louis, 119-20, 121-22,
    180
Cohen, Leonard, 158, 159-60,
    164-65
Comino, 35
Cominotto, 35
Coughlin, Bing, 128
Crosby, Bing, 11, 87
Curtis, Air Vice-Marshal W. A.,
    95, 111
Curtiss Rambler, 16
Cushing, Harry, 123-24

Daddo-Langlois, Raoul, 48-49
The Daily Express (London), 94
Davidson, Vic, 95
Dean, Basil, 129
Deflection shooting, 52, 53-56,
    155
de Marigny, Marie Alfred
    Fouquereaux, 118, 132
Demobilization, of Canadian
    servicemen, 130-31
de Niverville, A., 82, 88-89
Dewan, D. J. "Dewey", 107
Dickins, "Punch", 14
Donaldson, A. H., 52, 77-78
Donne, John, 126
Dunkelman, Ben, 142-44, 146,
    176, 180

Eagle, H.M.S., 39-40, 41-44, 46,
    48
Edward, G. G. "Gaff", 132
Edwards, Air Marshal H. Gus,
    96, 105
El Alamein, 38, 56, 66
Exclusive Brethren, 8-10, 29,
    173

Fighter planes:
    Cant bomber, 58
    Flying Fortress, 53
    Focke-Wulf 190, 31-32,
        100-01, 108
    Hawker Hurricane, 26, 27-28
    Junkers F-13, 13
    Junkers 88, 58, 71, 73
    Liberator bomber, 77-78, 79
    Macchi 202, 4, 55, 58, 64,
        83-84, 157
    Messerschmitt F-109, 38-40,
        55, 58-59, 101
    Norseman (C-64), 150-51,
        157, 158-60, 165-66
    Tiger Moth, 32, 104, 132-33,
        181
    Vickers-Supermarine
        Spitfire, 1-5, 27, 28-29,
        39-44, 57n, 68, 68n, 100-01,
        157
Filfla, 35
Fine pitch, 43
"Finger Four" formation, 57-58
Finland, Soviet invasion of, 23
Flight to Arras (Saint-Exupéry),
    126
Forte Antenna (Italy), 157, 159
Fuller, G. S. B., 113

Gardner, Diana Eve, 87–88, 115–25, 134, 135–36, 173, 180
Gardner, Edwin, 87
Gela (Sicily), 64
Gelli, Faliero, 64–66, 181
Giannini, Ferrero, 159, 164, 179
Gibbs, Hetty Florence. *See* Beurling, Hetty Florence
Gibraltar, 33, 36, 37, 39, 41–43
Gibson, Colin W. G., 129
Glenn, John, 14
The Globe and Mail (Toronto), 91, 156, 162
Godefroy, Hugh, 98, 100–01, 103–05, 181
Gozo, 35, 65
Grampian Mountains, 25
Grant, Stan, 40, 48, 55–56, 60, 61–62, 63, 179
Guerrini, Massimo, 156, 159, 164

Haganah, 138–39, 141, 144, 149
Haifa (Israel), 174
Hamilton, Frank, 136
Hartmann, Erich, 184
Haymarket Club (London), 94
Hendon (England), 24
Henry Hudson Hotel (New York), 149, 151, 153–54
Hiroshima, 130
Hitler, Adolf, 35–40 *passim*
Hogan, Ted, 15–16
Holderness, H. H. C., 25–26, 180
Holgate, Edwin Headly, 181
Hyndman, Robert, 97, 97*n*, 177

Imperial Oil, 13

Jacquemain, 131
Jodl, Alfred, 127-28

Johnson, Jean, 92
Johnson, Johnnie, 96, 99, 100, 109, 180
Johnson, R. O., 117
Johnstone, Ken, 131

Kappa, Umberto, 156
Keats, John, 126, 172, 173
Keith, Ron, 132
Kemp, Hugh, 117–18
King George VI, 61, 92
"The King of Lampedusa", 158
King, Prime Minister Mackenzie, 77, 79–81, 86, 95, 106

Lacey, Ginger, 30
Langley, Smith, 18–19
Larocque, A. L., 17
Lasalle Airport (Quebec), 15
Lawrence, T. E., 14
Leckie, Air Marshal Robert, 113
Leggo, Douggie, 71
Len Foggen Flying School, 20
Lewis, Philip, 74–75
Lindbergh, Charles, 14–15
Litvak, Lieutenant Lilya, 187
Lucas, P. B. "Laddie", 46–50, 52, 60, 61, 62, 63, 65–66, 71, 96, 179, 181
Luftflotte II, 38–40
Luftwaffe, 23, 73, 157; *see also* Fighter planes
Luqa (Malta), 66, 77
Lynch, Charles, 86

Machal (Mitnadvei Hutz Laa'retz), 137–51
Malta:
   British tactics for the defence of, 56–57

civilian response to RAF in, 60–61
colonization of, 36
geographic details of, 35–36
King George VI bestows George Cross on, 61
origins of inhabitants, 35–36
Rommel's campaign in, 37–40, 56
service life in, 1–5, 36–37, 45–75
"Malta Dog", 62–63, 67, 70
Malta Spitfire (Beurling and Roberts), 29*n*, 116
Mandel, Sidney, 138
Manoir Pinoteau, 122
Marlowe, Christopher, 126
May, "Wop", 14
McCrae, Bill, 108
MacKenzie, Andy, 99, 109, 179
McLean, Harry, 14
Maclean's, 134, 145, 147, 168
McNair, Robert "Buck", 47
Mdina (Malta), 46, 51, 67–75
Méditerranée (Rome), 154
Merritt (British Columbia), 19
Miles Master, 26
Mizzi, Enrico, 60–61
Mont-Tremblant (Quebec), 122–24
Montgomery, Bernard Law, 38
Montreal (Quebec), 7
Montreal Press Club, 140
The Montreal Standard, 145
The Montreal Star, 79, 81, 162
Montrose (Scotland), 25
Mount Royal Hotel (Montreal), 124–25, 131, 142–43, 148
Murphy, David, 10, 11, 12, 127
Murphy, Dolly, 10, 11–12, 116–17, 127

Murrow, Edward R., 149
Mussolini, Benito, 35, 37, 64

Nagasaki, 130
New Liberty, 136, 145, 168
Noorduyn, Robert, 151
Notre Dame de Grâce (Montreal), 161–62
Nyhuus, Jack, 154–55, 154*n*, 179–80

Oakes, Sir Harry, 118
O'Brien, Andy, 94, 117
Ohio (tanker), 70
Operation Overlord, 96–97
Operation Pedestal, 70

Palestine:
    expiry of British mandate in, 137, 148
    Israeli independence and, 156–57
    partition of, 136–37
    see also Arab–Israeli War (1948), Haganah, Machal
Pantelleria, 44
Paradis, Joseph, 60
Parioli (Rome), 173
Park, Air Vice-Marshal Keith, 73–74
Piermattei, Marcello, 172–73
Plymouth Brethren. *See* Exclusive Brethren
Pointe St. Charles (Quebec), 8
Poland, German invasion of, 21
Portland, Oregon, 22
Power, Charles Gavan "Chubby", 105
Public Archives of Canada, 83, 181

Quebec Conference (1943),
96-97
Queen Elizabeth, 91
Queen's Own Rifles, 142
Quirinale Hotel (Rome), 171

Rabat (Malta), 46
Raymond, Air Vice-Marshal,
112
"Rhubarbs", 102
Roberts, Leslie, 29, 29*n*, 116
Rockliffe Airport (Ottawa), 79
Rommel, Erwin, 2, 37-40, 56,
66, 70
Roosevelt, Franklin D., 39-40
Rouyn (Quebec), 18
Royal Air Force (RAF), 1-5,
23-24, 82, 92, 147, 169,
183-84, 186
Initial Training Wing, 24-25
No. 5 Elementary Training
School, 24-25
No. 8 Service Flying School,
25-28
Operational Training Unit
No. 57, 29
41 Squadron, 31-33, 48, 95
249 Squadron, 105, 47-64,
68*n*
403 Squadron, 30-31, 96-106
Volunteer Reserve, 24-33
Royal Canadian Air Force
(RCAF), 21-23, 82, 88-89,
95, 110, 111-14, 129-30,
175, 175*n*, 183-85
No. 3 Training Command,
111-12
412 Squadron, 106-10
Royal Canadian Corps of
Signals, 139

Royal Navy, 37, 70; *see also*
Eagle, H.M.S.
Royal Norwegian Air Force,
155

Sainte-Adèle (Quebec), 117-18
Sainte-Marguerite (Quebec),
119-24
Saint-Exupéry, Antoine de, 135,
177; *see also Flight to Arras*
Saint-Sauveur-des-Monts
(Quebec), 140
St. George's Anglican Church
(Montreal), 117
St. Paul's Bay (Malta), 67
Santo Spirito Hospital (Rome),
169
SAS (Scandinavian Airlines),
154-55
Scofield, Jack, 112*n*
Sea Island Airport (Vancouver),
20
Shelley, Percy Bysshe, 126, 172,
173
Sherbrooke Airways, 132, 134
"Sherut Avir", 150
Shulemson, Sydney, 138-40,
143-45, 146, 148, 149,
155-56, 161, 172, 176, 180
Sims, Edward H., 184
Skene, Joyce, 109
Smith, Rod, 141, 146, 147
Spoon River Anthology
(Masters), 135
Stokes, Sylvanus, 123
Stokes, Vivian "Vivi", 122-24,
125-27, 134-35, 145-46,
151-54, 162-63, 169-70,
171-74, 176-77, 178, 180
Straus, Oscar, 121

Sullivan, Ed, 162
Sun Life Assurance Company, 131

"Tail-end Charlie", 31
Takali Airfield (Malta), 1–5, 45–67, 180
Tales of the South Pacific (Michener), 149
Tallman, Frank, 69–70
Terrebonne (Quebec), 10, 127, 132, 181
Tiber River (Italy), 157–60
"Tiger Squadron", 63
Tilley, Reade, 63
Time, 162
Tuck, Summerville Pinkney, 147
Turner, Stan, 57, 72

Udet, Ernst, 22–23
Urbe Airfield (Rome), 156, 157–60, 163, 166
U. S. Air Force Museum, 165
U. S. Eighth Air Force, 96
U. S. Federal Aviation Agency, 165

Valletta (Malta), 4, 37, 61, 62
Valparaiso, 23–24
Verano Cemetery (Rome), 170, 172–73
Verdun (Quebec), 7–12, 181
Verdun Auditorium, 81–84
Victory Loan Drive (1942), 74, 83, 86–87, 88

Walker, Inspector P. S., 133
Wartime Information Board, 91
Wasp, U.S.S., 39–40

Waugh, Evelyn, 37
Wehrmacht, 37
West, Bruce, 71, 91, 93, 94, 156, 162
Western Canada Airways, 13, 14, 14n
Whittall, Diana Eve. *See* Gardner, Diana Eve
Wilson, Edward, 82
Windsor Hotel (Montreal), 81
Wright-Patterson Air Force Base, 165

Xara Palace (Mdina), 46, 67–75, 181

The Yogi and the Commissar (Koestler), 126

Zahal Cemetery (Haifa), 174
Žatec (Czechoslovakia), 157